H. W. BRANDS'S

AMERICAN PORTRAITS

The big stories of history unfold over decades and touch millions of lives; telling them can require books of several hundred pages. But history has other stories, smaller tales that center on individual men and women at particular moments that can peculiarly illuminate history's grand sweep. These smaller stories are the subjects of American Portraits: tightly written, vividly rendered accounts of lost or forgotten lives and crucial historical moments.

H. W. BRANDS

The Murder of Jim Fisk
for the Love of Josie Mansfield

H. W. Brands is the Dickson Allen Anderson Centennial
Professor of History at the University of Texas at Austin.
He was a finalist for the Pulitzer Prize in biography for
The First American: The Life and Times of Benjamin Franklin
and for *Traitor to His Class: The Privileged Life and Radical
Presidency of Franklin Delano Roosevelt.*

www.hwbrands.com

The Murder of Jim Fisk

for the Love of Josie Mansfield

The Murder of Jim Fisk

for the Love of Josie Mansfield

A Tragedy of the Gilded Age

AMERICAN PORTRAITS

H. W. BRANDS

Anchor Books

A DIVISION OF RANDOM HOUSE, INC.

NEW YORK

AN ANCHOR BOOKS ORIGINAL, JUNE 2011

Photo section credits: Picture History: p. 1; Library of Congress:
pp. 2, 3 (bottom), 4 (bottom), 5, 8; National Archives: p. 3 (top);
New York Public Library: pp. 4 (top), 6, 7.

Library of Congress Cataloging-in-Publication Data
Brands, H. W.
The murder of Jim Fisk for the love of Josie Mansfield : a tragedy
of the Gilded Age / H. W. Brands.
p. cm.–(American portraits)
ISBN 978-0-307-74325-1 (trade pbk.)
1. Fisk, James, 1835–1872–Assassination.
2. Fisk, James, 1835–1872–Relations with women.
3. Capitalists and financiers–United States–Biography.
4. Murder–New York (State)–New York–History–19th century.
5. Mansfield, Josie. 6. Showgirls–United States–Biography.
7. New York (N.Y.)–Biography. 8. New York (N.Y.)–Social life and
customs–19th century. I. Title.
CT275.F565B73 2011
974.7'103092–dc22
2010051174

Book design by Rebecca Aidlin
Author photograph © Marsha Miller

www.anchorbooks.com

Printed in the United States of America
10 9 8 7 6 5 4 3 2 1

The Murder
of Jim Fisk

for the Love of Josie Mansfield

 **1**

A gray blanket cloaks the trees of Montparnasse on a late autumn morning. Smoke from the coal fires that heat the homes and shops along the narrow streets swirls upward to join the fog that congeals intermittently into drizzle. This part of Paris hides the signs of the Great Depression better than the blighted industrial districts, but the tattered storefronts, the shabby dress of men with nowhere to go, and the age of the few cars that ply the streets betray a community struggling to keep its soul together.

An old, oddly configured vehicle lumbers slowly along the cobbles. The dispirited pedestrians pay it no mind. Nor do they heed the two women and one man who walk behind it. The women appear to be locals; the shawls around their shoulders and the scarves on their heads could have been taken from the woman selling apples on one of the corners they pass or from the grandmother dividing a thin baguette among her four little ones. (Or could she be their mother? Hard times play evil tricks on youth and beauty.)

The man must be a foreigner. He dresses like an Englishman, one whom the Depression seems to have spared. His heavy wool coat and felt hat shield him from the damp; the coat's collar and the hat's brim hide his face from those around him. He might be an American; he walks more assertively than the average Englishman. He probably walked still more assertively when he was younger, although how many years have passed since that sprightly era is impossible to say.

The two women speak quietly to each other. Neither addresses the man, nor he them. The vehicle—whether it is a car or a truck is as much a puzzle as most else about this small procession—slows almost to a stop, then turns onto the leaf-strewn lane of the cemetery that these days forms a principal raison d'être of the neighborhood. It moves tentatively along the track, picking its way among the gravestones and mausoleums, beneath the connecting branches of trees left over from when the farm on this site began accepting plantings that didn't sprout, not in this existence. The driver finally locates what he has been looking for, and he stops beside a fresh pile of dirt that is gradually turning dark as the drizzle soaks in. Two men shrouded in long coats suddenly but silently appear, as if from the earth itself. They stand at the rear of the vehicle as the driver lowers the gate. They grasp handles on the sides of the bare wooden box the vehicle contains, and with a nonchalance just shy of disrespect they hoist it out and set it on the ground between the pile of dirt and the hole from which the dirt has come.

They step aside, wordlessly letting the three mourners know that this is their last chance to commune with the deceased. One of the women produces, from a cloth bag, a small cluster of chrysanthemums and places it on the coffin. The man takes a rose from inside his coat and, with quiet tenderness, lays it beside the other flowers.

The three step back and gaze down at the wooden box. The drizzle turns to rain. The gravediggers slip short loops of rope inside the handles and lower the coffin into the grave. They pull up the ropes and begin shoveling the dirt back into its hole.

The hearse drives away, at a faster pace than before. The women walk off together. The man lingers. He looks at the grave, then at the city in the distance, then back at the grave. Finally he too departs.

2

Another day, another decade, another funeral. And such *a* funeral. Lifelong New Yorkers cannot remember larger crowds, even to mark the Union victory in the Civil War. Many of those present today attended the victory celebration, but it is the nature of life in the great city, and the strength of the city's appeal to outsiders, that a large part of the population has turned over in the seven years since the Confederate surrender at Appomattox. Today the newcomers crane to see what the fuss is about.

The funeral begins at the Grand Opera House on Twenty-third Street, where the body has lain for viewing. No one thinks the choice of venue odd—or at least none thinks it odder than that the Opera House is also home to one of America's great railroads, the Erie, of which the deceased was a director and to which he, as owner of the Opera House, rented office space. The lavish interior of the house—the sweeping grand staircase, the twenty-foot mahogany doors embellished with the company initials "E. R.," the bronze horses pawing the air furiously with their forehooves, the two-story mirror with the bust of Shakespeare on top, the sumptuous wall hangings, the carved and gilt columns, the cherubs disporting about the ceiling, the fountains spewing water into the air—has been rendered somewhat more somber for the sad occasion by the addition of black muslin tied up with black and white satin rosettes, to cover the cherubs and hide the gilt.

The visitors have been gathering since dawn; by eleven, when the doors open, they number ten thousand. They file slowly in, some entering by the door on the Twenty-third Street side, the others from Eighth Avenue. They approach the rosewood casket with its gold-plated handles. They see the deceased in his uniform as colonel of New York's Ninth Regiment of militia. His cap and sword rest on his chest; his strawberry curls grace his forehead and temples. His face appears composed, albeit understandably pale; to some this seems strange, given the circumstances of the death. Flowers of various kinds—tuberoses, camellias, lilies—cover the lower portion of the body and surround the casket. Their scent fills the gallery. An honor guard of the Ninth Regiment stands at attention.

First to view the body are the other directors of the Erie Railroad and certain members of the New York bar and judiciary. When the general public is let in, several women professionally associated with the opera—of which the deceased was a prominent patron—burst into tears. His barber stops at the head of the casket and, with one hand, rearranges the curls while, with the other, he twists the tips of the dead man's moustache.

As the last of the visitors depart, the funeral service commences. The chaplain of the regiment reads from the Episcopal prayer book. The wife, mother, and sister of the deceased, all veiled and dressed in black, sit quietly for the most part, only now and then airing a sigh or an audible sob. At the end of the reading, each of the women approaches the casket and kisses the dead man. The rank and file of the regiment march slowly past their fallen comrade and commander, paying silent tribute.

The casket is closed and covered with an American flag. The honor guard carries the casket to a waiting hearse. The regiment's band, backed by musicians from one of New York's German associations, tolls a dirge.

The funeral procession forms up. One hundred New York policemen take the lead, followed by the band, which has segued into "The Dead March in Saul." A contingent of employees of the Erie Railroad come next, un-uniformed except for the black crape that adorns their arms. The full regiment, in parade dress, marches in triple file behind the Erie men. The hearse, pulled by four caparisoned black horses, rolls at a stately pace. A Negro groomsman guides the colonel's favorite horse, a snorting black charger. The saddle is empty; reversed boots fill the stirrups. Officers of New York's other regiments trail the stallion. Distinguished civilians, in handsome carriages, bring up the rear.

The procession moves slowly east on Twenty-third Street. Businesses have closed out of respect for the dead man's passing; curtains and shades have been drawn on the private residences. Onlookers pack the sidewalks and spill into the streets. Others stand in the doorways and open windows of the buildings and on every balcony and stoop. Most are respectfully silent, but children shout and strangers who don't know why the city has come to a midday halt insistently ask. More than a few of those familiar with the irreverence of the deceased talk and laugh in a different form of respect.

The procession turns north at Fifth Avenue. The regiment corners smartly, the others at their whim. Two blocks bring them to the New Haven depot, where a locomotive and train stand waiting. The pallbearers transfer the casket to a special car, draped in black, attached to the rear of the train. The family and close friends climb aboard the car to accompany their loved one to his final resting place in his native Vermont.

The locomotive puts on steam and slowly pulls the train out of the station. No one departs until the train has gone. "And thus passed from sight the mortal remains of one who might have been a vast power for good, had he made use of the glorious opportunities vouchsafed to him," an eyewitness, more knowledgeable and literary than most, remarks. "Doubtless he had noble qualities, but they were hidden from the eyes of men, while his vices seemed to be on every man's lips."

3

Yet another day, another decade, another spectacle. Of course,
every day with Jim Fisk is a spectacle. Or so Josie Mansfield often observes.

Josie knows as much about Fisk as anyone does, and
more than most people do. She knows he comes from
Vermont, where he mastered the arts of persuasion
while peddling tools and trinkets to the closefisted
farmers of the Green Mountain State, whose wives loved
Fisk for bringing the civilized world to their doorsteps
and whose children thought of him as Santa Claus.
She knows that he moved from Vermont to Boston in
search of wealthier customers and fatter profits, and from
Boston to New York for the same reason, amplified. She
knows—or at least has heard—how he made a fortune
smuggling Southern cotton to Northern mills during the
Civil War.

She knows he loves a spectacle, and that the spectacles

he loves best put him at center stage. He perfumes his hair and waxes his moustache; he wears velvet coats of peacock colors, tailored low in front to reveal the diamond studs in his silk shirts. More diamonds, much larger, adorn his fingers and sparkle when he twirls the fat cigars he employs to punctuate his florid sentences.

Josie knows Fisk runs with a fast crowd on Wall Street. He is Dan Drew's protégé and Jay Gould's partner; the three speculators have joined forces to fight the formidable Cornelius Vanderbilt for control of the Erie Railroad. Drew's domed forehead and beetled brow hide secrets of market manipulation vouchsafed to few in the financial world; his starched collar and tight cravat cover a heart that can merely be presumed to exist. Many on Wall Street swear Drew invented the double cross; more reliable authorities make him the pioneer of stock watering, which he is said to have adapted from the days when, as a cattle drover, he herded beeves down Broadway and swelled their bellies with water before unloading them on naïve purchasers. Now he simply dilutes the value of corporate stock by issuing new, sometimes bogus shares. The Erie is Drew's special plaything, his favored vehicle for manipulation. Josie can recite the Wall Street triplet: "Daniel says up, Erie goes up / Daniel says down, Erie goes down / Daniel says wiggle-waggle, it bobs both ways." Yet Drew combines conscienceless weekday practice with weekend piety; he never misses Sunday service at the Fourth Street Methodist Church and is endowing a divinity school to propagate the Gospel and bolster the Golden Rule—to repair the damage he does it during the week, Drew watchers suggest.

She knows less about Jay Gould, in part because Gould cultivates mystery. He hides his comparative youth—he is not quite thirty-two—behind a bushy black beard and in public defers to Drew and Fisk. But his dark eyes flash when speculation is afoot, and his unconscious habit of tearing paper to shreds while reckoning risks and rewards tells Josie, whose biography has taught her to read men, that *he* might be the one to watch out for.

Cornelius Vanderbilt is the titan of Wall Street—full of ambition, even at seventy-three years of age; full of money, as the wealthiest man in America; full of himself, with flowing white hair and sideburns that suit his imperious manner. He won his fortune by strength of will and often of arm; broken jaws and black eyes among the competition marked his rise to the top of the world of steam transport. He built a fleet of passenger ships and still insists on being called "Commodore"; lately he has diversified into trains. He drives the fanciest coach in Manhattan, pulled by the fastest horses and filled with the prettiest young women. His wrath is legendary and his wealth gives him the power to wield it. "Gentlemen," he famously wrote to a cabal who crossed him, "you have undertaken to cheat me. I won't sue you, for the law is too slow. I'll ruin you." And of course he did.

He similarly aims to ruin Drew, Fisk, and Gould, who stand between him and control of the Erie Railroad. Josie knows that if Vanderbilt joins the Erie to his New York Central Railroad he will possess a monopoly of freight and passenger traffic between New York City and the Great Lakes and will become even wealthier, more prideful, and more powerful than he already is. The city and much of the Eastern Seaboard will be in his grasp; millions will pay whatever charges he deigns to dictate. If he fails to gain the Erie, he will gnash his teeth in the frustration he always feels at being bested and likely will launch a counterattack that could rock the railroad industry to its roots. With the economy as a whole coming to depend on railroads—these days hardly anything or anyone moves more than a few miles without riding a train—the fate of the country may rest on the outcome of the battle for the Erie.

Josie and New York watch as the strategies of the two sides unfold in early 1868. Vanderbilt's assault is characteristically frontal: he orders his brokers to buy all the Erie shares they can. Like many frontal assaults, Vanderbilt's attack is expensive: each round of purchases drives up the share price. But Vanderbilt's great wealth almost guarantees success, and he intends to recoup his investment by hiking the Erie's rates and fares after he captures the road.

Drew's defensive strategy is likewise characteristic, in his case deviously so. Drew currently commands a controlling interest in the Erie, and he has lately added Fisk and Gould to the board of directors, which authorizes the issue of $10 million in bonds convertible to stock. The function of the bonds, Drew tells the board, is to fund improvements to the road; in reality he plans to use them against Vanderbilt. Together with some stock shares authorized by the board but not yet issued, the bonds give Drew potential access to some 100,000 shares that the market—meaning, at this point, primarily Vanderbilt—knows nothing about.

Vanderbilt's ignorance is crucial to Drew's plan, for the fate of the Erie turns on the question of whether Vanderbilt will run out of money before Drew and his comrades run out of stock. The share price continues to mount as the Commodore presses his purchasing, but Vanderbilt, allowing for the shares known to exist, calculates that he can absorb the rising price and still reach his goal.

Stealthily Drew, Fisk, and Gould engage a printing house to produce new stock certificates. These are blank forms, which the three fill in with the appropriate dates, amounts, and signatures. The operation brings a smile to Drew's dour countenance; even the ebullient Fisk has never had such fun. Fisk merrily pronounces their operation an example of "freedom of the press." When Gould warns him not to count his money too soon, Fisk laughs. Vanderbilt is as good as beaten, he declares. Even the Commodore's great fortune can't stand the weight of the new shares. "If this printing press don't break down,"

Fisk promises, "we'll give the old hog all the Erie he wants."

The next day they spring their coup. Vanderbilt is still buying confidently when the first of the secret shares enter the market. The brokers, feeling the crispness of the paper and smelling the freshness of the ink, realize that these are new and heretofore unaccounted for and that Vanderbilt is in serious trouble.

The Commodore grows furious at Drew's maneuver, which at a stroke dilutes the value of the shares he has acquired, frustrates his attempt to seize control of the Erie, and embarrasses him for not having anticipated Drew's ploy. "Damn the innocent face of that old hypocrite," he thunders. "I'll whip him if it costs me a leg." He goes to court and obtains an injunction to disallow Drew's new shares and prevent Drew and the Erie directors from issuing any more.

Now it is Drew's turn to register offense. The courts have no place in the matter, he declares. Besides, New York's courts are notoriously corrupt and Vanderbilt's enjoining judge, George Barnard, is the worst of the bunch. Drew alleges that Vanderbilt has purchased his injunction.

Drew's indignation doesn't prevent him and Fisk and Gould from enlisting a judge of their own. The task isn't easy, for Vanderbilt's reputation and money have touched the ermine all around New York. But eventually they find a court in Binghamton willing to endorse their interpretation of corporate law: that the Erie directors can issue new shares of stock at will.

The market in Erie shares is a shambles. Vanderbilt presses forward, buying as fast he can and striving to prop up the price. Drew, Fisk, and Gould keep cranking out new shares, forcing the price down. Smaller investors, whipsawed between the main contenders, run for their lives.

Vanderbilt returns to Judge Barnard's court. The friendly jurist approves a warrant for the arrest of Drew, Fisk, and Gould, for violating his earlier injunction to stop issuing stock. Vanderbilt smiles in prospective triumph; there is no printing press in the Ludlow Street jail.

Drew and the others learn almost at once that the sheriff is on the way. In the financial world, where knowledge is money, news travels fast—by the couriers who have long carried messages about the city, by the telegraph lines that increasingly link brokers to banks to corporate headquarters, by the spies all self-respecting speculators employ, and sometimes, it seems, by the mere nervous energy that pervades Wall Street and its environs. Fisk tells Drew and Gould how Vermonters sought by the law sometimes skip across a bridge over the Connecticut River into New Hampshire and from the far side snap their fingers in defiance at their pursuers. The Hudson is broader than the Connecticut and no bridges yet span its channel, but it might serve a similar purpose.

The three quickly gather their uncirculated stock certificates, the Erie ledger books, and $7 million in cash, much of it drained from Vanderbilt for the watered stock, and head for the Hudson. A policeman stops them on West Street, wondering at their hurry and the bags of money they're carrying. Fisk assures him that all is well; they are simply relocating the offices of the Erie Railway. He tips the patrolman five dollars for his vigilance, and the grateful copper lets them pass.

They race to the landing where the Erie operates ferries to supplement its rail lines. They consign their baggage to one of the cargo handlers. Then Fisk, with surprising insouciance even for him, turns to go back into the city. He says he wants to say a proper good-bye to his friends. Gould prepares to accompany him. Drew tells them that they're crazy and that he is too old to risk a night in jail. Besides, he isn't about to let the company's records and cash out of his sight.

The ferry pushes off. Drew doesn't yet relax. He understands that the limit of New York's jurisdiction lies in the middle of the Hudson, and he fears that Vanderbilt will intercept him before he gets there. But the passage proceeds uneventfully, and he lands in Jersey City a free, if still wanted, man.

He settles into a suite at Taylor's Hotel, close to the ferry terminal. He watches the afternoon ferries arrive, expecting with each one to see Fisk and Gould step off. But daylight fades and evening sets in, and there is no sign of them.

Finally, well past dark, the two appear, in a bedraggled state. Gould is typically taciturn, but Fisk tells the story. They took a cab from the ferry terminal on the New York side to Delmonico's restaurant for a farewell luncheon, he says. Word of their presence spread, as did reports of the disappearance of Drew. The sheriff serving the Vanderbilt-orchestrated arrest warrant discovered their location and approached the entrance to the restaurant. Fisk and Drew fled out the back. They briefly considered taking the Erie ferry across the Hudson but surmised that Vanderbilt would have men posted at the terminal. So they ventured to a rival line and paid the captain of the vessel in the slip for the use of a lifeboat and two oarsmen. They jumped in, and the rowers pulled the small craft away from the shore. Fisk directed them to row upstream, away from the regular track of the Hudson ferries. But night was falling, accompanied by a thick fog, and they found themselves rowing in circles. Out of the fog a ferry suddenly materialized; their rowboat was nearly run over. They seized the side of the ferry and let it haul them through the water, realizing amid the roar of the engines and the violent splashing from the bow wave that if their grip failed, they would be swept to the stern and splintered in the ferry's paddle wheel.

But somehow they held on and reached New Jersey intact. When they arrive at Drew's suite in Taylor's Hotel, Gould is shaken and haggard. He complains that their ignominious flight has ruined their reputation in New York. Fisk is as wet and unkempt as his partner, yet his face is rosy and he treats the scrape as a lark. The $7 million in Drew's valise affords all the comfort he requires.

4

Almost *all the comfort, rather. Josie Mansfield provides the* rest.

She hadn't expected to move to Jersey City; she was getting to like New York. But she supposes she'll survive, if the exile isn't permanent.

She has learned to adapt, having no alternative. Her mother, who named her Helen Josephine, took her from Boston, where she was born, to gold rush San Francisco. Her father disappeared early, replaced, as a male figure, by a stepfather and then a husband. Of the stepfather she speaks as little as possible, apparently trying to remember as little as possible. Her husband, Frank Lawlor, was an actor whose finest role, in the judgment of the fifteen-year-old Josie, was rescuing a damsel in distress, namely her. The marriage got her out of California but didn't do much for her emotionally or otherwise, and she and Lawlor agreed to part. She returned to

Boston, found little to sustain her there, and moved to Philadelphia. She liked Philadelphia but heard fascinating stories of New York, ninety miles up the Pennsylvania Railroad. The Civil War was over; business in the great city was booming, and men with money needed women with charm.

Josie doesn't lack charm, although precisely what it consists of, in her case, sometimes eludes description. She isn't classically beautiful; her nose is too long, her jaw too square. But her brown hair flows in waves and her heavy-lidded blue eyes exert an irresistible attraction on male eyes, even pulling them away from her voluptuous form.

She is familiar, from Frank Lawlor, with the theater; she knows that it affords opportunity for attractive but impecunious young women. To the New York theater she goes. She calls herself an actress, a category comprising all manner of strivers, from prostitutes to mistresses to honest-to-goodness stage players. Josie lands midspectrum, although she aspires to the more respectable end of the scale.

In her aspiration she finds Jim Fisk. She occasionally visits the Thirty-fourth Street establishment of Annie Wood, a former actress and current madam, and in November 1867 notices Fisk, of the jeweled fingers and the fancy clothes. She whispers to Annie that she'd like an introduction, and Annie obliges.

Josie can tell at once that Fisk is smitten. She can

always tell such things. She lets him admire her. Their eyes meet; Fisk can't take his away.

She confesses to him that she knows almost no one in this strange city. When he responds as sympathetically as she supposes he will, she apologizes for her plain and well-worn dress, saying it is the best she can afford. When he inquires where she lives, she says in a modest rooming house but that she might not be staying there long. Why? he asks. Because the rent is due and she is short, she replies. Within the hour he becomes her protector and provider, and she his fond friend.

Within the week he decides that she requires better lodgings. He finds her a room in a more respectable boardinghouse. He visits her there and the friendship blossoms. He buys her dresses and diamonds. He eventually purchases her a house, a stylish brownstone on Twenty-third Street not far from his own house.

He drops over during the day and most evenings. He brings friends, and she entertains them. He and the friends talk business; she listens. She asks him questions about his speculations; hearing his answers, she praises his cleverness. She inquires, hesitantly, whether she might participate in some of his safer endeavors. He delightedly consents. She laughs with pleasure and bestows kisses and other signs of affection when her investments succeed.

She knows of Mrs. Fisk, and that she lives in Boston, but she and Fisk don't speak of her. When Fisk travels to

Boston she accepts his explanation that it is for business, just as she accepts the presents he brings her when he returns.

She sometimes visits him at the office. She can tell that the visits annoy Dan Drew and Jay Gould, who obviously disapprove of her and her relationship with their partner. But she knows that Fisk likes to show her off. And anyway, a girl of twenty-two has to get out now and then.

She is surprised when he informs her, in March 1868, that he will be staying in Jersey City for a while. She has been observing the struggle with Vanderbilt, but she hasn't imagined it would come to this. When he invites her to join him at Taylor's Hotel and says it will be like a vacation, she considers her options and decides to stand by her man. For now.

5

Josie's arrival prompts Drew to reconsider his partnership with Fisk. In New York he can ignore most of Fisk's improprieties, but Jersey City is a small town, and Taylor's Hotel is even smaller. Josie's fleshly presence affronts him, and when she and Fisk disport themselves like newlyweds on a honeymoon, Drew has to wonder where Fisk's priorities lie. Drew attempts to improve the moral tone by attending a nearby church, but the example doesn't take, and Fisk and Josie carry on as before.

The continuing confrontation with Vanderbilt doesn't help Drew's mood. Drew imagines that Vanderbilt will try to kidnap him and carry him back to New York's jurisdiction; the Commodore has played rough before. So Drew has Fisk and Gould arrange security measures. They persuade the Jersey City police chief to position a special detail around the hotel; to this they add precautions of their own. Fisk hires four boats with a dozen armed men each to patrol the approaches to Jersey City lest Vanderbilt mount an amphibious assault. He enlists dozens more men from the gangs of the neighborhood to stand guard outside and within the hotel, which he jokingly dubs Fort Taylor.

The formidable appearance and dubious character of the impromptu Erie militia make Drew wonder whether the cure isn't worse than the disease. He increasingly blames Fisk and Gould for his predicament. The stash of money aggravates the strain. Drew considers the $7 million his, since he is the principal shareholder of the Erie and the originator of the scheme by which the money has been acquired. Fisk and Gould believe *they* have a claim to substantial shares of the loot, as partners in the operation. They know Drew's reputation for double-dealing; they request, then demand, their portions, which Drew declines to cede. The conspiracy starts to unravel.

And so, even as the trio entices the New Jersey legislature into incorporating the Erie as a New Jersey company, to make Vanderbilt think they might *never* return to New York, Drew gets word to the Commodore that he wants to make peace. Fisk and Gould are alert to such a defection, and Fisk monitors all mail, telegrams, and other messages entering and leaving the hotel. But Drew bribes a waiter to get a note past Fisk, and a meeting with Vanderbilt is scheduled.

One Sunday Drew leaves the hotel as if for a Sabbath stroll. Out of sight he slips to the waterfront, where a waiting boat carries him across the Hudson. Not trusting Vanderbilt, he has deliberately chosen Sunday, when arrests in civil cases are suspended. He takes a cab to Vanderbilt's home in Washington Square. Drew attempts small talk as an icebreaking courtesy; Vanderbilt gruffly gets to the business at hand. They agree that the Erie war has lasted long enough, and they accept the need for a settlement. No details are discussed, and Drew remains edgy. He watches the clock, knowing that if he is still in New York at midnight, he risks being arrested. But he gets away from Washington Square in midevening, and he is across the Hudson before his skiff turns into a pumpkin.

Yet Fisk and Gould have noted his absence and divined his destination. When he returns they declare emphatically that they expect to be included in any subsequent negotiations. Drew explains that he was simply trying to look out for their interests—better than they could themselves, as he has been in the speculating game longer than they have. They don't believe him. They watch him closely, and when he seems to be preparing to go back to New York again, they insist on joining him.

He still manages to lose them. He says that the meeting is at the Fifth Avenue Hotel but that he has to make a stop before going there. They should proceed; he will meet them. He turns instead toward the home of former judge Edwards Pierrepont, where Vanderbilt is waiting.

The two principals reach an agreement. Drew will

retain control of the Erie and will keep the profits he has made on the run-up in the company's share price, but the Erie will buy back the watered stock he and Fisk and Gould have sold Vanderbilt. Both sides will abandon their legal proceedings.

Drew and Vanderbilt are about to seal the pact when Fisk and Gould burst into the room. Vanderbilt roars with laughter to see Drew's deception uncovered by his partners. Drew forces a smile and affects not to be upset. He asks Fisk and Gould to join the discussion. The terms are delineated.

Fisk balks at buying back Vanderbilt's shares, complaining that it will cost the Erie millions. But Gould pulls him aside. They whisper together. Then they return to the table, and Gould, who till now has let Fisk do the talking, says he and Fisk will accept the deal on one condition: that Drew turn control of the company over to them.

Now Drew balks. He has gotten rich from the Erie, and he is loath to lose the chance to get richer still. But he is also reluctant to reopen the battle with Vanderbilt, who bellows delight at Drew's discomfiture. And he realizes that Fisk and Gould can outvote him if the matter comes before the Erie directors. So he takes his money and walks away from the company, appreciating the irony that he has saved the Erie from his rival only to lose it to his friends.

 **6**

Josie is happy to return from Jersey, and even happier when Fisk announces a new home for the reconstructed management of the Erie. Samuel Pike has opened an opera house on Twenty-third Street at Eighth Avenue; its ornate design and elaborate furnishings draw the attention and patronage of the theater set in the city. But Pike encounters cash flow troubles and hints that he might have to sell. Fisk has been an impresario at heart since youth; it tickles his ambition to imagine himself the proprietor of an opera house, with all the opportunities for self-promotion proprietorship entails.

Gould is skeptical, wondering what an opera house has to do with running a railroad. But Fisk's excitement inclines Gould to believe that the Opera House will keep Fisk busy, leaving Gould to manage the company. He assents to Fisk's plan, which calls for purchasing the Pike place and refitting the second floor to be headquarters of the Erie.

The railroad is one of the state's largest employers, and the New York papers report the relocation as a major event. Some applaud the move to larger quarters as overdue; others question the extravagance even by the generous standards of the Gilded Age. The same papers carry a simultaneous announcement that the Erie is building a new ferry terminal at the foot of Twenty-third Street, just a few blocks from the Opera House. Proximity to the Erie offices is one consideration; another is readier access to the railroad stations of midtown. The Erie will operate a horse railway from the ferry to the Opera House and the stations, ensuring the swiftest travel for its customers. Observers of the late flight to Jersey cheekily remark that the new arrangement will also facilitate fast getaways for the Erie directors, should the necessity again arise.

The possibility appears quite real. Dan Drew leaves the road literally a wreck: in the week of his departure an Erie night express from Buffalo careens off rails that were supposed to have been replaced with fresh ones funded by money he is discovered to have diverted to his own pocket. Four cars plunge over a cliff, somersault several times, burst into flames (from upset stoves employed to heat the cars), and wedge into the bottom of a narrow canyon, trapping the passengers, twenty-two of whom burn horribly to death. The "Erie Slaughter," the papers call it, and it reminds the public—and the new Erie directors—that a railroad is a serious business, not simply the plaything of speculators.

Yet Fisk can't take anything very seriously for long.

He lets Gould run the Erie and revels in his role as master of ceremonies at the renamed Grand Opera House. He entertains more lavishly than before, hosting pre-performance receptions and post-performance suppers for special guests and members of the casts.

Josie is often on his arm and in his personal box. She mingles with professional actresses and dancers, who swirl about Fisk as though he is the most important, powerful, and attractive man in New York. The presence at the Opera House of other important men—elected officials, judges, business associates—tends to confirm the impression. Champagne flows freely; cigar smoke clouds the air. The Opera House has many private rooms where Fisk's guests can get to know one another better.

Fisk visits these rooms, but he ends most evenings at Josie's house, just around the corner. It is his home away from home, and he spends more nights there than in his own house—and many more nights than he spends at the Boston home of Mrs. Fisk. Moralists like Dan Drew shudder at Fisk's flouting of the conventional code, but in his own way he is the soul of domesticity. Josie will remark how often he comes home—that is, to her house— in the evening and promptly falls asleep, too exhausted from playing the Prince of Erie, as the papers call him, to do any of the scandalous things ascribed to him.

On these nights she looks around her house, at her dresses and diamonds and furniture and paintings, and concludes that she has done well for herself. And yet, as her eye falls on Fisk, slumped in an armchair with his coat thrown off, his stomach bulging over his belt, his jowls hiding his cravat, his snores shaking the paintings and the silver, she wonders if there isn't more to a young woman's life.

7

William Tweed enjoys the company of Fisk and Josie at the Opera House and often at Josie's afterward. He feels an affinity with Fisk as another who has climbed from humble beginnings to the top of his profession—New York politics, in Tweed's case. Like Fisk he displayed an early flair for persuasion, talking friends into forming the Americus Fire Company No. 6, a volunteer unit that branched out from firefighting to other worthy activities. His Manhattan neighbors voted him their alderman in the decade before the Civil War, and then their congressman. But his heart remained in his home city, and after two years in Washington he returned to New York, where he sat on the board of supervisors before being elected to the New York state senate in Albany. His most important positions, however, have always been with the political machine that controls Democratic politics in New York City. He has a gift for the rough-hewn politics of urban democracy; his intuition tells him what people want and need, and what they are willing to pay for it. He has cultivated friends and fought off rivals until, in the half decade after the Civil War, he becomes the master of Tammany Hall, as the Democratic machine is universally known, for one of its gathering spots. By virtue of his leadership of Tammany, Bill Tweed is among the most powerful men in America's largest and richest city.

To the respectable classes of New York, Tammany stands for everything that is corrupt in politics. It blatantly buys the votes of poor immigrants, paying for them with goods and services furnished from public funds. Tweed and his Tammany ring don't deny that they help themselves to the spoils of politics, but they contend that victors have a right to the spoils. Besides, they say, they are the agents of democracy, taking men where they find them, even in the gutter, and bringing them to the altar of American politics, the polls on election day. Someone has to set the Irish and other immigrants on the path to assimilation, and who better than Tammany?

Yet Tweed has been testing the limits of the city's tolerance of graft. Contractors complain not so much at having to kick part of their compensation from the city back to Tweed and his cronies; this has long been standard practice in New York. But the size of the bribes required to do business with the bosses has grown dramatically under Tweed, till the contractors wonder if the returns on their payments make Tammany's patronage worth the trouble.

Editors and other keepers of the public conscience complain that Tweed is selling out the general interest to please
the Irish, the immigrant group that forms the predominant
element of the Tammany coalition.

Tweed can stand the criticism, but like Jim Fisk he
appreciates diversions from his day job. He first encountered Fisk and Gould at the end of the Erie war against
Vanderbilt, when the two entreated Albany for prefer-
ment for their railroad. Tweed answered their entreaties
and in exchange received a position on the Erie's board
of directors.

The relationship serves both parties. The Erie directors get Tweed's help on matters of law and politics.
When the Erie needs permission to lay new track or
build a depot, when the Erie wants a change in its corporate charter, when the Erie requires a favorable judicial
ruling, Tweed and Tammany deliver. Tweed and his
cronies receive advice on investing from two of Wall
Street's best-placed insiders, and direct payments from
the Erie treasury when cash is needed. As the speculators
and the politico confer behind the oak doors of the Erie
offices, as Fisk and Tweed share Fisk's box at the Opera
House and Fisk's whiskey at Josie's—the abstemious
Gould stays home with his wife—they spin a web of reci-
procal influence. The Erie circle and the Tweed ring
overlap and interlock; what strengthens one strengthens
the other, what threatens one threatens both.

 **8**

By 1869 Jay Gould is a full-blooded railway man. He is rumored to be a full-blooded Jew as well. As his facility with money becomes apparent, his rivals put out that his name was Jacob Gold before he anglicized it. He ignores the rumors as he considers how to boost the Erie's central business: transporting freight and people. He devises a plan that depends on a financial vestige of the Civil War: the paper dollars that circulate alongside America's gold dollars. The former, called greenbacks for the color of their ink, rise and fall in value compared with the gold dollars, which are paper too but are backed by the federal Treasury's promise to redeem them in gold, unlike the nonredeemable greenbacks. The greenbacks, being legal tender but less valuable than the gold dollars, predominate in the domestic American economy; the gold dollars are employed in international trade. A rise in the value of gold relative to greenbacks translates into cheaper American exports, especially of farm products from the West, and hence more of them. More exports mean more traffic on the Erie. Gould therefore favors a rise in gold.

During the summer of 1869 he talks up gold to private investors, who express interest but lack especial influence, and to government officials, who possess influence but, at first, little interest. He and Fisk make friends with Abel Corbin, the husband of President Grant's sister. Corbin arranges a meeting with Grant, during which Gould and Fisk point out the benefits to the American people in general and the Erie Railroad in particular of healthy exports. "We have employed on the Erie road some twenty thousand men, all told, and a stock of eight hundred locomotives, with the other equipments of the road on a corresponding scale," Gould tells Grant. "I am aware of no way in which these men and equipments can be used to advantage unless the crops come forward from the West." Grant is noncommittal but appears inclined to let the market find its own price for gold, without the government's getting involved.

Gould cultivates the assistant federal treasurer in New York, Daniel Butterfield, who oversees the government's gold trades. Butterfield's is a critical position, for the federal Treasury contains sufficient gold to move the price substantially up or down, depending on whether the government is buying or selling. Butterfield doesn't set policy, but he implements it, and he will know before anyone else in New York if Grant changes his mind and orders the government to intervene in the gold market.

Gould himself begins buying gold, discreetly but decidedly. He uses multiple brokers and keeps his own hand hidden. He hopes to create a broad surge that will feed on itself and move the gold price higher.

At some point his plans grow larger. From the devious Drew and the daunting Vanderbilt he has learned the concept of a "corner," a market anomaly in which more of a commodity or stock has been contracted for sale to a purchaser—the cornerer—than exists on the market. The sellers find themselves at the mercy of the cornerer, who can dictate terms of settlement. Corners in wheat, pork bellies, railroad stocks, and other assets have been attempted and occasionally accomplished on Wall Street; Gould now develops a scheme to corner gold. If successful, the operation will make Gould very wealthy. It might also paralyze the financial system, but Gould leaves that problem to others.

Gould writes the script but remains in the shadows; Jim Fisk takes the production to center stage. In late September Fisk barges into the Gold Room, the special market at New Street and Wall where gold and greenbacks are frenetically traded. Regulars in the Gold Room liken it to a gambling parlor or a dog pit; the marble Cupid in the center should be a Midas, some say, turning everything to gold and starving in the process.

The latest innovation is a mechanical indicator of the

current price. A large arrow responds immediately to rises and falls in the dollar value of gold. On the morning of Friday, September 24, the arrow rests at 143, indicating that 143 greenbacks are required to purchase 100 gold dollars. When the Gold Room opens at ten, the arrow likely will creep upward, as it has been creeping upward since the first of September. Gould's quiet purchases of gold have boosted the price; market watchers and players, including speculators who have climbed on the Gould bandwagon and become gold bulls, expect the rise to continue.

Yet something strange is afoot. Gold brokers have crowded the curb outside the Gold Room since dawn, and transactions are already taking place. A broker bids 145; his offer is accepted. Another bids 147; also taken. By the time trading officially begins, the price has topped 150. The gold arrow leaps the 5 percent—a large amount in this context—all at once.

And it keeps moving upward. Violent emotions surge across the Gold Room: the money lust of the gold bulls, who see their speculation nearing success and shout for the price to go still higher; the incipient panic of the gold bears, who have bet on a fall and now stare ruin in the face.

Amid the maelstrom stands Jim Fisk. His cherubic face beams with the pleasure of a child at play, an image rendered a bit incongruous by the cigar with which he punctuates his shouts at the brokers. In the stifling atmosphere of the Gold Room he is sweating profusely; the salty rivulets have plastered his strawberry ringlets to his forehead and caused the waxed ends of his moustache to droop. Fisk loudly and belligerently leads the charge of the gold bulls against the bears. As the price rises past 150, he bawls to his brokers: "Take all you can get."

The price leaps upward again; the big arrow on the gold indicator lurches to 155. The Gold Room explodes in shouting, arm waving, and rushing to and fro. The anarchy sloshes next door to the stock exchange, where share prices have been heaving up and down on the hopes and fears of the gold men. One broker, more agitated than most, vows mortal harm to a nearby gold bull, promising to shoot him dead if he persists in driving gold up. The bull responds by tearing open his shirt and inviting the bear to fire. Fisk roars with delight and goads the bears further. "Take all you can get at 160!" he shouts above the din.

The bears see their end fast approaching. Most are already insolvent; their only hope is that the corner will break and the price fall before their creditors can catch them. This last hope fairly vanishes when the price jumps again, to 162.

And then . . .

The weak link in the golden chain of Gould and Fisk has always been the gold reserve of the government. Should this gold be released on the market—should the government in Washington even signal an intent to release it—the corner will be broken. This is why the partners have urged the president to keep the government out of the market, and why they have cultivated Butterfield as a lookout in the Treasury Department.

Grant has withheld the government's hand till now, not wishing to intervene in a contest among the capitalists. But the wailing of the bears has carried to Washington by telegraph, and finally the president becomes alarmed, fearing that a gold corner will trigger a financial collapse. Shortly before noon on this Friday, he orders the Treasury to sell.

The order, relayed to New York, hits the Gold Room like a thunderclap. At noon, by the first chimes from the steeple of Trinity Church, the neighborhood outpost of Episcopalianism, where winning brokers offer thanks and losers pray for deliverance, the gold arrow hovers in the 160s; only moments later, before the echoes of the last of the dozen peals has faded, the arrow has plunged to the 130s.

The bears, lately strangling on their fears, suddenly breathe the fresh air of salvation. Again they see the sun; once more they feel the earth beneath their feet.

It is the bulls' turn to panic. Great riches were in their grasp a moment ago; these have been snatched away. And because most of their purchases have been made with borrowed money, accepted at extortionate rates, the evaporation of their golden dream now threatens them with utter dissolution. As the new reality sets in, their groans of disappointment turn to howls of fear and rage.

The bulls look to their leader, Fisk, for guidance. But Fisk has vanished. Some claim to have seen him dashing north toward the Opera House. A small herd of angry bulls give chase; they shout that if they catch Fisk, his carcass will swing from one of the lampposts that line Broadway.

The mob reaches the Opera House, where they crash against a wall of thick men retained by Fisk and Gould for such emergencies. The jagged scars and flattened noses of the men suggest they have dealt with desperadoes more threatening than disappointed brokers. The mob mills around, wondering what to do.

Inside the Opera House, behind the heavy doors of the Erie office, Fisk wipes the sweat from his face and reclaims his composure. Gould greets him in a calm, low voice, apparently oblivious to the uproar outside. But his fingers work with subtle fury, tearing odd sheets of paper into tiny bits. While Fisk mops his brow, Gould carpets the floor around his desk with confetti. Separately and silently they calculate how they'll survive this latest debacle. "It was each man drag out his own corpse," Fisk will say of the moment. "Get out of it as well as you can."

 **9**

Love makes the most careful man reckless. Nothing else can explain Jim Fisk's decision to introduce Edward Stokes to Josie Mansfield. Ned Stokes is the ne'er-do-well son of a New York family that used to be rich but currently must send its sons to work. Stokes supervises a Brooklyn oil refinery that the family controls and that Fisk, on behalf of the Erie, acquires an interest in. Fisk takes a liking to Stokes, who is seven years younger than Fisk, seventy pounds lighter, and incomparably more handsome, in a darkly dangerous way. Any sensible man in Fisk's position would keep Stokes as far from Josie as possible. But Fisk arranges a meeting between Stokes and Josie, and he later takes Stokes to Josie's house to further the acquaintance.

He seems not to notice the spark between the two— a spark that becomes an electrifying surge as soon as Fisk looks away. Stokes has a wife, a child, and a more regular domestic existence than Fisk, but thoughts of home and hearth fly out of his head when he sees Josie. She has stuck with Fisk from considerations of financial security and perhaps a mite of gratitude, but security has brought boredom, and any gratitude she feels toward Fisk melts away when Stokes kisses her hand and gazes deeply into her eyes.

Fisk is busier than usual, these months after the gold panic. The brokers and investors who wanted to lynch him and Gould on the afternoon of what is being called Black Friday are burying the two in lawsuits; Fisk spends half his waking hours with attorneys. Congress wants to know how the gold conspiracy nearly succeeded and who in the Grant administration was involved; Fisk spends the other half of his time testifying before committees in Washington.

He doesn't realize that Stokes has become a regular visitor to Josie's house. More fatigued than usual in the evenings, he doesn't observe that Josie is happier than she has been for some while, but in a distracted, distant way.

10

Fisk grows busier all the time. After the Erie war and Black Friday, he reckons that his civic reputation can use some burnishing. When a delegation from the moribund Ninth Regiment of the New York National Guard approaches him about becoming their sponsor, he listens closely. Regimental enrollment is down, the envoys explain; uniforms are shabby; the armory is ancient. All this might change should Jim Fisk lend his support. They would be honored to recommend him to the rank and file for election as colonel of the regiment.

The idea intrigues him. The pomp and pageantry of soldiering have always appealed to him. A steamboat line he owns lets him playact an admiral, but the National Guard is the real thing. During the Civil War he followed the custom of the financial classes in shunning enlistment while letting the draft fall on those who couldn't afford to hire a substitute or pay the $300 commutation fee. The invitation from the Ninth Regiment seems a chance to reap the honorific benefits of service without crimping his business activities or facing the hazards of combat. If the men of the regiment become so loyal to their commander as to guard him against his personal enemies, all the better.

"I'm no military man," he tells his interlocutors. "I've never trained a day in my life, never shot off a gun or pistol, and don't know even the ABCs of war, yet. Fact is, I doubt whether I could shoulder arms or file left, or make a reconnaissance in force, or do any of them things, to save my boots. And as for giving orders—why, I don't know anything about it." But he supposes he can learn. "Elect me, and then we'll talk about it." The men of the Ninth excitedly elect him, and he and they talk about all those matters, and others more immediate. He buys them uniforms, furnishes food and drink on weekend excursions, and outfits the regimental band with new instruments. The Ninth, lately the laggard of the New York regiments, becomes the pride of the city. Fisk offers $500 to the regimental company that enlists the largest number of fresh recruits; the resulting competition causes enrollment to double.

Fisk determines to present his regiment to the city, and he can think of no better venue than the Opera House. The hall is crowded on a Saturday night in May 1870; the staging of *The Twelve Temptations* has drawn enthusiastic reviews. The curtain is late in rising, and the management has offered no explanation. The atmosphere grows oppressive; the ladies and some men fan themselves to catch a breath.

Suddenly, just before nine, a commotion is heard outside the theater proper, in the foyer. Necks crane and eyes scan the doors. To no one's great surprise, Fisk emerges as the source of the hubbub. He enters the hall, dressed in the full regalia of his colonelcy. Behind him, two by two, enter the five hundred men of the Ninth Regiment, stepping lively to the accompaniment of the regimental band. Fisk has saved the best seats for the soldiers, most of whom give the appearance of never having been inside such a theater. Awkwardly and noisily they find their places.

Fisk beams, proud to show off his theater to his regiment and his regiment to the patrons of his theater. The audience, skeptical at first, allows itself to become part of the spectacle and offers rousing applause to these defenders of the state and their doughty commander.

Yet one man bucks the tide of good cheer. A constable with a summons makes his way to Fisk, in the presence of the regiment and the regular audience. He hands the colonel the notice that he must answer to the authorities for an outstanding debt. Fisk scans the summons and with theatrical disgust tosses it to the floor. He proceeds to his personal box.

The constable tries to follow Fisk, but several members of the regiment's Company K, which deems itself

Fisk's personal bodyguard, block the way. One of the men retrieves the summons and reads it aloud. Messrs. McBride and Williams, grocers, have sued the colonel for alleged delinquency in paying for seventy-five pounds of butter. The total due is $41.25. The audience roars at the incommensurability of the present grand celebration and the measly butter bill. Fisk dramatically glowers and declares that his enemies are trying to upstage him.

The curtain rises and the scheduled performance begins. Fisk watches the opening act and then repairs to the lobby to greet late arrivals and, at intermission, the rest of the house. He issues directions to the waiters who circulate among the crowd dispensing champagne. He shakes hands with the gentlemen, bows to the ladies, and slaps the backs of his men. At the conclusion of the performance he leads the officers of the regiment into one of the private rooms for a late supper. More champagne mingles with stronger spirits. The officers toast their colonel's health and generosity; ribald references are made to Messrs. McBride and Williams and the unredeemed butter.

11

In the summer of 1871 Bill Tweed finds himself in a quandary. New York's battling clans of the Irish are at it again, and the Tammany boss is caught in the middle. Protestant Orangemen from Northern Ireland want to parade: to commemorate the victory of William of Orange over Catholic Irish nationalists in the 1690 Battle of the Boyne and to insult the descendants of those Catholic nationalists here in New York. Last year's Orange parade produced a murderous confrontation between the Orangemen and the Catholic Irish in which eight people died and many were injured. Tweed has tried to avert a reprise by ordering Mayor A. Oakey Hall and police superintendent James Kelso to deny the Orangemen a parade permit for this year.

But the ban evokes angry protests. A meeting of merchants at the Produce Exchange approves a resolution decrying the "imperious and illegal order" and deprecating "this utter violation of the rights of the people." The *New York Herald* declares the ban a fateful step down a slippery road to the kind of repression currently manifested by the radical Commune in Paris, where blood has flowed in the streets and much more seems likely to flow. The *Times* taunts Tweed, Hall, and Kelso for bowing to the Irish: "City Authorities Overawed by the Roman Catholics." The same paper prints a letter to the editor demanding, "It is Pope or President for this country," and "Have Americans any rights now?" The letter's author signs himself "Old Vet of 1812" and gives his place of residence as "Ireland (late New York)."

The outcry compels Tweed to reconsider. He confers with Governor John Hoffman, who has come down from Albany, and they direct Mayor Hall and Superintendent Kelso to rescind the ban. The government will not prevent the Orangemen from marching. On the contrary, Hoffman says, the government will enforce the Protestants' right to assemble and march: "They will be protected to the fullest extent possible by the military and police authorities."

Now the Catholic Irish protest, in their own, direct fashion. In the early morning of Wednesday, July 12–Orange Day–police discover an effigy hanging from a telegraph pole in front of the liquor store of Owen Finney at 14 Spring Street, not far from Hibernian Hall, the headquarters of New York's militant Irish. The figure is made to look like a man dressed in orange. The police cut the figure down and inquire among the neighbors as to who might have hoisted it. No one offers any information, with most seeming sullen and others fearful.

Inside Hibernian Hall a large crowd of Catholics gathers to denounce Tweed and the authorities for reversing the no-parade policy. An undercover journalist has infiltrated the meeting and records the angry oaths. "This is the governor *we* elected," one protester sneers of Hoffman. The crowd plots a countermarch of its own. Someone suggests demanding a police escort, lest the marchers be attacked. Another person, more attuned to the spirit in the hall, retorts, "We got arms enough and can do our own fighting." This elicits loud applause, and a question: "Where are the arms?" The man chairing the meeting, a Mr. Doyle, answers: "There will be enough arms here in half an hour to arm all that are present." Another man shouts: "How about the volunteers?" Chairman Doyle replies: "We shall have thousands join us when we march out. Arrangements have been made that they shall be supplied if they want them."

At this point some notice that the covert journalist isn't responding with the zeal of the rest. "Reporter in the room," the chairman bellows. "What are you doing here? We don't want you." The next day's paper will summarize the journalist's response: "The reporter, knowing the impulsive nature of the Hibernians, wisely concluded to leave the hall and in this way escaped the personal violence which he heard threatened as he went down the stairs."

The reporter encounters soldiers and police deploying rapidly around the city: "There was hurrying, in hot haste, of armed men through the streets converging to the several points of rendezvous of the National Guard and of large companies of police officers hurrying to their head-quarters at the Central office. It was as if a deadly enemy of the Commonwealth was expected at the gates, and an alarmed people were making hasty preparations for defense. But when it was considered that the enemy was within the community, and that it was an arrogant faction determined by force to deny to others the liberty which it claimed for itself, and that all these preparations were necessary to enforce the laws against those who swore to obey them, every reflecting citizen saw that the crisis was more portentous than if a foreign fleet were bombarding the City, or a foreign host at its gates."

The Catholic Irish naturally interpret the situation differently. The Orangemen are provocateurs, they claim, shielded by the Protestant-intimidated establishment. The provocateurs must be punished. Irish workers drop their tools and walk off their jobs all across the city— quarrymen from a construction site at Tenth Avenue and Forty-sixth Street, longshoremen from the docks at the foot of Houston Street, rail workers from the Third Avenue line, thousands of laborers from myriad other sites. Many come willingly; some, threatened with instant dismissal by Protestant employers, have to be taunted or intimidated into joining the swelling crowd of Irish protesters.

They meet their women and children on both sides of the Orange parade route, along Eighth Avenue above Twenty-first, in time for the early-afternoon start. They fill the sidewalks several rows deep and jam the intersections at the cross streets. They taunt and curse the police and militia who precede the marching Orangemen; many hurl rocks and bottles along with their imprecations. The patrolmen and soldiers suffer the bombardment for a time, but then the police charge the mob, laying about with billy clubs, and the soldiers fire blank rounds of warning. Whether the blanks provoke live fire from the mob or are simply followed by real rounds from the soldiers' muskets will furnish grist for years of debate; today the question is lost amid the smoke and shrieks that rise above the gun reports and the collision of thousands of angry bodies.

No one counts the dead today; survivors are too busy trying to escape the line of fire and bludgeon. Tomorrow coroners and local hospitals will tally some sixty bodies and twice that many wounded. Shopkeepers will wash the blood and gore from around their entryways. Patrick Ford's *Irish World* will condemn the "Slaughter on Eighth Avenue" and the Irish neighborhoods will seethe with resentment at the Orangemen and those who took their side. A grand jury headed by foreman Theodore Roosevelt, whose twelve-year-old son, also called Theodore Roosevelt, has observed the violence from the safe distance of the family's Union Square home, will congratulate Governor Hoffman for taking action that proved "a necessity to preserve the honor of our city." Police commissioner Henry Smith, a friend of Roosevelt's, will wonder whether the police and militia should have responded with even greater force. "Had one thousand of the rioters been killed," Smith will say, "it would have had the effect of completely cowing the remainder."

The one thing the two sides agree on is that Bill Tweed is a miserable excuse for a civic leader. In the papers, in meeting halls, on street corners, they pound him unmercifully. The Irish Catholics condemn him as a coward for bending to the Protestants; the Protestants damn him for incompetency in failing to prevent the Irish violence.

12

The pummeling drives Tweed closer to Jim Fisk, a rare New Yorker agnostic on the Irish question. Fisk has his own Orange Day story. "On Tuesday night, about twelve o'clock," the colonel of the Ninth Regiment explains, "I called on Governor Hoffman and Mayor Hall at Police Headquarters and had an interview with those officials in reference to my regiment in the coming trouble. During our powwow I informed the Governor that in case of a riot I expected that the Twenty-third Street Ferry and the Grand Opera House would be assailed by the mob. His Excellency concluded to let the Ninth Regiment protect both places. There being a rumor that a body of Orangemen intended crossing the Twenty-third Street Ferry"—from New Jersey—"to take part in the New York procession, it was decided that should such an attempt be made, the ferry boats should be withdrawn, and they should not be permitted to cross. Governor Hoffman thought he should have enough to do to protect his own people, and was not willing to become responsible for the safety of those belonging to any other city or state."

Fisk was ready the next day. "About midday a messenger arrived from the Grand Opera House with the information that a large number of men were crossing the Twenty-third Street Ferry. I immediately went to the Opera House and sent for Jay Gould. I wanted to know of him if the charter"—of the Erie Railroad—"would be violated by stopping the ferry boats. Not being able to find Gould, I took the responsibility upon my own shoulders and telegraphed to Mr. McIntosh, the agent at Jersey City, to stop running the boats. My order was at once obeyed."

Meanwhile the Ninth had been mustering at its armory to join the procession in order to protect the Orange marchers. A messenger brought word that the men were all in place. "I started out and began to walk back," Fisk explains. "As I approached Twenty-fourth Street, the crowd on the sidewalk hooted me and yelled at me." The Irish crowd knew Fisk as the commander of the Ninth and didn't like his protecting their historic foes. "I immediately took the middle of the street, and walked on in that way till I came in sight of the Sixth Regiment just ahead. In the meantime the crowd was gathering behind me, when all of a sudden I heard a shot and felt a bullet whiz past me. I went in the ranks of the Sixth, the crowd continuing their hooting until I got to my own regiment."

He had left his uniform coat and sword at the armory, but with the parade beginning he had to make do in shirt-sleeves and with a borrowed weapon. "I took the major's sword and assumed command. The procession began to march, and soon after we started a lot of bricks and stones were thrown at us, and in some instances shots were discharged. My men had received instructions before leaving the armory not to fire off their pieces until they should be assaulted by the mob, and not to fire if only stones should be thrown. But should it become so hot that they could not stand it, and should any shots be fired, they were not to wait for any orders, but were to fire into the mob and protect themselves.

"No attention was paid to the missiles until Walter Pryor was struck by a bullet in the knee, and Harry Page was killed. I was standing within a few feet of him. At that moment discharges of musketry were heard from the head of the line, and my men, becoming excited at the death of one of our best members, opened fire upon the mob. My regiment was a little distance behind the Sixth. The crowd on the east side of Eighth Avenue, into which the troops were firing, now came rushing between the two regiments. I was standing in front of my regiment with Major Hitchcock's sword in my hand. The mob closed in upon me in an instant, knocked me down, and trampled upon me.

"After the crowd passed me I tried to rise, and found I was hurt about the foot. I cannot say whether I was struck by anything, or received my injuries by being trampled upon. Some of my men, seeing my condition, carried me into a bakery close by. I was taken to the second story and the surgeons examined my foot and found that my ankle was out of joint. They took hold of it and jerked it back into place. The surgeons then left me, and as I was looking out of the window with Captain Spencer I saw the crowd close around the two men of my regiment who had been left in charge of Page's body. I saw a man make a thrust at one of them with a sword-cane.

"The next thing I remember was hearing an Irishman, who stood in front of the bakery, cry out, 'That damned Colonel Fisk is in here. Let's go in and kill the villain.' Others said, 'Hang him.' Crowds began to gather thick and fast about the door, and fearing that the house was about to be sacked, I seized a heavy cane which had been given me, and left by the back way. I must have jumped over five fences, when I reached a house through which I went, and attempted to pass out by the front door. Looking down the street toward Eighth Avenue, I saw the mob still there. Coming down Ninth Avenue was another crowd, a hard looking set. For a moment I thought there was no possible chance of escape, but on glancing across the street I saw a door open and ran toward it. This house is in Twenty-seventh Street, between Eighth and Ninth Avenues. I went through the hallway to the yard. Here I met a high fence. I found a barrel, mounted it, and climbed over. I climbed several more fences before I became exhausted at last, and started for a house fronting on Twenty-ninth Street. Some woman slammed the door in my face. Seeing a basement window open, I crawled into it, and was confronted by an Irishman, who wanted to know what it all meant. I explained my case to him, and borrowed a pair of old trousers, an old hat and a large coat. When I left the house, the crowds had disappeared from Twenty-ninth Street, having followed the procession down.

"My first thought was now for a carriage. Seeing none in sight I limped toward Ninth Avenue, and looking down the street I espied one coming up. I hailed the driver, and looking inside saw Jay Gould. The driver stopped, but Gould, not knowing me in my disguise, ordered him to go on again. I explained who I was, and was taken in. The driver took us to the Hoffman House; but I had not been there more than fifteen minutes before a mob collected around the neighborhood. Seeing that danger still followed me, I ordered another coach, and was taken to the Pavonia Ferry, where a number of our tugs are generally stationed. I got on board of one of them and was taken to Sandy Hook. From there I went to Long Beach in the cars. I did not take off my disguise until I reached the Continental Hotel."

13

Fisk's narrow escape doesn't impress Josie, who is too enamored of Stokes by now to remember what she saw in Fisk. Stokes reminds her: Fisk's money, which still supports her and, to the extent Stokes takes meals and amusement at Josie's, increasingly supports him. She calculates how she might rid herself of Fisk while retaining access to his money. She recalls Fisk making investments on her behalf, and how he would congratulate her when they paid off. Till now she has been happy to let her winnings ride and be reinvested; she hasn't even asked for an accounting. She remembers Fisk saying she is twenty or twenty-five thousand dollars to the good; she and Stokes estimate that such a sum might make her independent of Fisk.

Josie knows how to entice a man; she also knows how to dispense with him. She picks a fight through the notes they exchange when his business takes him away from her. "I never expected so severe a letter from you," she writes after a mild reproof. "I, of course, feel it was unmerited; but as it is your opinion of me, I accept it with all the sting. You have *struck home*, and I may say turned the knife around." She escalates, suddenly and dramatically. "I am anxious to adjust our affairs. I certainly do not wish to annoy you, and that I may be able to do so I write you this last letter."

The adjustment she refers to involves money. "You have told me very often that you held some twenty or twenty-five thousand dollars of mine in your keeping," she says. "I do not know if it is so, but that I may be able to shape my affairs permanently for the future, a part of the amount would place me in a position where I would never have to appeal to you for aught." She asserts her faithfulness, by her own lights. "I have never *had one dollar from any one else*." She seeks simple justice. "I do not ask for anything I have not been led to suppose was mine, and do not ask you to settle what is not entirely convenient for you."

Fisk responds as she intends. He recognizes that she is throwing him over. "The mist has fallen," he replies, "and you appear in your true light." She wants him to leave, and so he will. "Have no fears that I will again come near you." He encloses a ring she has given him— a ring purchased with his money. "Take it back. Its memory is indecent." He will pay her outstanding bills. "If there are any unsettled business matters that it is proper for me to arrange, send them to me, and make the explanation as brief as possible. I fain would reach the point where not even the slightest necessity will exist for any intercourse between us. I am in hopes this will end it."

He signs and sends the letter, only to realize he hasn't rebutted her claim for the money. He writes a second letter. He reminds her of how much he has spent on her, even after she stopped reciprocating his affections. "You will, therefore, excuse me if I decline your modest request for a still further disbursement of $25,000." He lets her know he is aware of her relationship with Stokes; the gossips have twittered it for months. A gentleman's pride and a hope that she would change her mind kept him from mentioning it, but now that it is in the open he relates something else the gossips have said: that Stokes has had to pawn personal possessions to cover debts. Fisk does not intend to redeem Stokes's goods for him. "I very naturally feel that some part of this amount might be used to release from the pound the property of others, in whose welfare the writer of this does *not* feel unbounded interest."

His tone remains distant and proper almost till the end of this missive, when his emotions pour out. "You say that you hope I will take the sense of your letter. There is but one sense to be taken out of it, and that is an epitaph to be cut on the stone at the head of the grave in which Miss Helen Josephine Mansfield has buried her pride. Had she been the same proud-spirited girl that she was when she stood side by side with me . . . she would not have humbled herself to ask a permanency of one whom she had so deeply wronged, nor would she stoop to be indebted to him for a home which would have furnished a haven of rest, pleasure and debauchery, without cost, to those who had crossed his path and robbed him of the friendship he once felt. . . .

"Now, pin this letter with the other—the front of this is the back of that—and you will have a telescopic view of yourself, and your character, as you appear to me today; and then, I ask you, turn back from pages of your life's history, counting each page one week of your life, and see how I looked to thee then, and ask your own guilty heart if you had not better let me alone."

She realizes she has pushed too far. She visits him and warms his heart once more. He writes in astonishment: "Who supposed for an instant that you would ever cross my path again in a spirit of submission? . . . You have done that you should be sorry, and I the same. . . . You acted so differently from your nature that I forgive you. . . . When your better character comes in contact with mine, we are so much alike. . . . All now looks bright and beautiful, and my better nature trembles at ideas that were expressed last night."

And yet he has to distrust his heart, for his mind understands he has lost her to another. "I can see you now as you were last night, when you talked of this man"—Stokes. "Do not deceive yourself: *you love him*. . . . Leave me alone; for in me you have *nothing* left."

So he says; she thinks differently. She plots with Stokes how they might force a settlement from Fisk. Stokes has read some of the letters Fisk has written her; he and Josie decide Fisk might pay a substantial sum to keep the letters from appearing in the New York papers.

Fisk responds with outrage to the mere suggestion. He will never yield to blackmail, he vows. He backs his promise with action. He spreads word of the attempted extortion, decrying the threatened breach of the inviolability of a gentleman's correspondence. He launches a lawsuit against Stokes, saying Stokes has tried to swindle him in some of their business dealings. To give bite to the suit, he arranges with a Tammany judge, an associate of Bill Tweed, to have Stokes arrested. He entices one of the servants from Josie's house into his own employ and pumps the young man for damaging information about Josie and her new paramour.

Josie counters with a lawsuit of her own. She demands the money she says he owes her, adding interest and costs for a total of $50,000. To support her case she sends the newspapers a letter she has recently written him, which the papers happily print. "You and your minions of the Erie Railway Company are endeavoring to circulate that I am attempting to extort money from you by threatened publications of your private letters to me," she declares. "You know how shamelessly false this is, and yet you encourage and aid it. Had this been my intention, I had a trunk full of your interesting letters, some of which I would blush to say I had received. If you were not wholly devoid of all decency and shame you would do differently—knowing as you do that when your own notes to my order are brought into the Courts, and your letters acknowledging your indebtedness to me, you will appear all the more contemptible and cowardly. . . . Do you in your sane moments imagine that I will quietly submit to the deliberate and wicked perjury you committed in swearing to these injunction papers? . . . Unfortunately for yourself, I know you too well and the many crimes you have perpetrated. . . . You surely recollect the fatal Black Friday. The gold brokers you gave orders to to buy gold, and then repudiated the same, because, as you said, they had no witnesses to the transactions. There was one I recollect in particular—a son of Abraham—who had the courage to swear out an attachment against the Grand Opera House for what was justly due him, and how you and Jay Gould ruined the poor victim by breaking up his business and having him arrested and imprisoned for perjury; and at the same time you premeditated this crime, you well know he held your written order to buy gold, and you were the perjurers."

She said nothing about Fisk's iniquities at the time, putting loyalty to him above fidelity to her conscience. But now he has turned on her and is trying to add her to the ranks of his victims, she says. "It is an everlasting shame and disgrace that you should compel one who has grown up with you from nothing to the now great Erie impresario, to go to the Courts for the vindication of her rights which you refuse to adjust for reasons you too well know. It is only four years ago when you revealed to me your scheme of stealing the Erie books. How you fled with them to New Jersey, and I remained there with you nine long weeks. How, when you were buying the Legislature, the many anxious nights I passed with you at the telegraph wire, when you told me it was either a Fisk palace in New-York or a stone palace at Sing Sing, and if the latter, would I take a cottage outside its walls, that my presence would make your rusty irons garlands of roses, and the very stones you would have to hammer and crack appear softer under my influence. You secured your Erie palace, and now use your whole force of Erie officials to slander and injure me."

She will not be so treated. "I write you this letter to forever contradict all the malicious, wicked abuses you have caused to be circulated." She says she seeks nothing but fairness and justice; she offers to settle out of court. But she doesn't expect him to accept her offer. "I only make this proposal to place myself in the proper light and spirit." If he insists on fighting, she will fight back. She knows he has friends in high places, but she won't be intimidated. "If you feel your power with the Courts still supreme, and Tammany, though shaken, still able to protect you, pursue your own inclinations; the reward will be yours."

Josie's public letter lifts her fight with Fisk to a new level. The correspondence in her possession involves not only Fisk and his failed love affair but the Erie Railroad and those involved in the struggle for its mastery, including high officials of Tammany Hall. Jay Gould has always avoided publicity; now the glare of popular scrutiny follows him everywhere. Bill Tweed, still staggering from the Orange Day riot, appears more vulnerable than ever. All New York takes note.

14

The lawyers mobilize. They launch additional suits and countersuits. They record depositions and file affidavits. They probe the political connections of judges in search of sympathetic venues. They furnish reporters with information damaging to their opponents and seek to limit the harm done by their opponents' releases.

The Fisk side produces a statement by Richard King, the servant lately of Josie's, who declares that he has overheard Josie, Ned Stokes, and Marietta Williams, Josie's cousin and housemate, discussing a plan for selling Fisk's letters to Josie to the newspapers or, alternatively, blackmailing Fisk to prevent the publication. "They said that they could get a large amount of money out of Mr. Fisk in that way," King testifies. He goes on to quote Josie as saying to Stokes: "I have the letters, and I will give them to you and let you use them to your best advantage and make all you can out of Mr. Fisk."

Fisk sues Josie and Stokes for blackmail, citing the King statement, and applies for an injunction to bar publication. A judge who owes his position to Bill Tweed grants Fisk the injunction.

Josie retaliates with a libel suit against Fisk. "Each and every one of said conversations are false and untrue," she swears. Her lawyers publish an affidavit from another servant, Maggie Ward, who claims that Fisk offered her inducements to say what King had said: that Josie and Stokes were trying to blackmail him. "I told Fisk that I would not swear to anything of the kind for the whole Erie Railroad," Miss Ward says, "as it would be wholly false, wicked and untrue, and he knew it." She adds that Fisk asked her what she thought of King's affidavit. "I told him I thought it was awful, and he ought to be ashamed of himself for getting King to make such an affidavit. Fisk then told me I had better tell Miss Mansfield, if I were a friend of hers, to stop making affidavits or drawing papers against him or she would get into great trouble."

In filing their lawsuit, Josie's lawyers have chosen their venue wisely. Judge Butler Bixby, presiding over the Yorkville Police Court on the Upper East Side, is a foe of Tweed and Tammany. He signs out an arrest warrant against Fisk and sets bail at $35,000.

The Yorkville arrest clerk carries the warrant to the Opera House. The business of the Erie has gotten Fisk and Gould arrested numerous times; they keep a bail bondsman on staff. Fisk glances at Josie's warrant and hands it to the bondsman, who prepares the bond for Fisk's signature. The transaction—arrest, bond, bail—takes but minutes.

The suit goes to trial in November 1871. A large and rowdy audience fills Judge Bixby's Yorkville court. The demeanor of many of the visitors and the tone of their responses to the testimony suggest a connection to the Erie Railroad, and reporters soon ascertain that Fisk has granted a paid holiday to workers who report this morning to the courthouse instead of the roundhouse.

Josie arrives on time, with Marietta Williams. Fisk comes late, resplendent in his military uniform. He is accompanied by his attorneys, William Beach and Charles Spencer. Josie's counsel, John McKeon, sits beside Assistant District Attorney John Fellows, who has joined Josie's lawsuit on grounds that libel is a crime and Fisk needs to be convicted of something.

McKeon opens for Josie's side with what will prove a theme of the trial: the assertion that Fisk, far from being the fun-loving, even clownish Prince of Erie, is really a dangerous man. Anyone who crosses him, man or woman, does so at hazard to health and limb. "I know the risk a man runs by opposing Mr. Fisk," McKeon says. "A man's life is in danger." But Fisk has finally met his match. "I mean to tell him, and he may sneer at it, the day may come when some developments may be made which will shock this community. Mr. Fisk will find at least one man that cannot be intimidated."

As the court and the audience ponder the meaning of this statement—who is the man that will not be intimidated?—Josie is summoned to the witness stand. She relates how Richard King was stolen away from her. "He left my employment without giving any notice whatever. I returned home one afternoon and found he had left."

District Attorney Fellows reads King's affidavit alleging the blackmail conspiracy. "Now, Miss Mansfield, will you state whether the conversations here alluded to ever took place?" Fellows asks.

"Never in this world," Josie replies.

Was there anything true in King's allegations, or were they entirely false?

"False in every particular."

Fellows thanks the witness and turns her over to Fisk's attorney for cross-examination.

Charles Spencer asks her how old she is.

"I will be twenty-four years of age on the 15th of December next, and have resided in this city since 1867. I resided immediately previous in Philadelphia."

"Are you a married lady?"

"I was married in San Francisco, in 1864, to Mr. Frank Lawlor. I had not been previously married. I only resided in San Francisco a few months. I married in September, and left on the 11th of January following."

"Have you any recollection, Miss Mansfield, while you were in San Francisco, of Mr. Lawlor's placing a pistol to a man's head?"

The question takes Josie by surprise, and the audience as well. She looks plaintively to the judge, who offers no assistance. "Never to my knowledge," she says hesitantly.

"Have you any recollection of a pistol being placed at a man's head in your presence?"

She appears pained but determined. "Well," she says, "I can't tell unless you tell me by whom, because I don't remember."

District Attorney Fellows objects to this line of questioning as irrelevant.

Spencer responds that he is testing the credibility of the witness. In a case of alleged blackmail, he says, he ought to be able to question the general truthfulness of the plaintiff.

Fellows rejoins that the plaintiff's past personal life has nothing to do with the case at hand. Her marriage, her divorce, and anything pertaining to those, he says, should be excluded.

Spencer reiterates that the credibility of the witness is crucial to her charge of blackmail, as it is a matter of her word against Fisk's—and King's.

Judge Bixby accepts Spencer's arguments and lets the questioning proceed.

"Can you not tell me whether in San Francisco a pistol was pointed in your presence at a man's head?" Spencer asks again.

"There was a circumstance of that kind," Josie answers.

"Was it a man by the name of D. W. Pearly?"

"Yes, sir."

"Was it pointed at him by a person of the name of Warren?"

"Yes."

"Where was Pearly at the time?"

"In the parlor of my mother's house."

"Did he sign a check before he went out?"

"Yes."

"For how much?"

"I have not the remotest idea."

"Did you hear the amount mentioned?"

"No."

"Was there any relation subsisting at the time between yourself and the person called Warren?"

"He married my mother."

"Any between yourself and Mr. Pearly?"

"None whatever."

"When Warren called and found Pearly inside, what did he say?"

"I don't remember."

"Do you recollect Warren coming into the room and charging Pearly with being criminally intimate with you, and telling him he must either be shot or pay?"

The audience is hanging on every word. Stories of Josie's past have made the rounds in New York; these have included tales of her work as an "actress" in San Francisco and of an abusive stepfather. But those in attendance today suddenly surmise that Josie's stepfather pimped her out and threatened at least one of her clients with blackmail.

Josie is obviously distressed and flustered. "Nothing of that kind passed at all," she insists. But then she contradicts herself. "I don't remember anything about a check. Warren did not shoot Pearly. Pearly left through the door."

Spencer takes advantage of her discomfiture. "Did he have anything on him except his shirt?"

"He was fully dressed."

Spencer gives her a skeptical look. He lets the image of Josie and her john and her stepfather-pimp, with the gun of the stepfather leveled at the john, who pays his tab before fleeing the scene of the illegal liaison, sans pants, linger in the courtroom for several moments.

Spencer then asks Josie to explain where she got her divorce.

"I got divorced from my husband in New York state," she answers. "The divorce was signed by Judge Barnard. My husband was served with notice of the divorce in this city."

Spencer asks how Josie met Fisk.

"I first saw him in the house of Annie Wood, in Thirty-fourth Street. She was an actress, and an acquaintance of my husband."

"When you became acquainted with Fisk, had you any property?"

"A little."

"How much personal property had you, outside of your personal ornaments?"

"I might not have had a bank book, but I certainly was not poverty stricken. I have always been well cared for."

"You appear to be," Spencer says, nodding knowingly. Some in the audience laugh. "How much personal property did you have at this time?"

Josie's lawyers object, and the question is excluded.

Spencer ascertains that Josie lived at the America Clubhouse after meeting Fisk. "During the time you resided at this clubhouse, did Fisk pay your board?" he asks.

"No, sir, not to my knowledge, nor did he make me any presents individually."

"Did he directly or indirectly furnish means for you while you were at the clubhouse?"

Josie turns to Judge Bixby. "Am I obliged to answer that question?"

The judge responds that she is not required to say anything that will incriminate or disgrace her.

"Did he, directly or indirectly, furnish means for you while you were at the clubhouse?" Spencer repeats.

"He did not personally contribute to my support, but it was through him I made some money, through some speculations. I don't, of course, think that he supported me. I did not understand it so. It was not done with that intention at all."

The audience listens closely and, by the dubious looks

on many faces, disbelievingly as the kept woman denies her keeping.

Spencer articulates the room's doubts. "Do I understand you to say that when you were at this clubhouse you were supported through money received from stock operations conducted on your behalf by Colonel Fisk?"

"Yes, it was to that effect."

"What were these stock operations?"

"They were some entered into by a mutual friend of ours—Mr. Marston."

"Who furnished Marston money for the operation?"

"I don't know who furnished him with the money. I suppose it was his own."

"Did you ever receive money from Marston or Fisk as the proceeds of that stock operation?"

"Yes, sir, two or three hundred dollars a month."

Heads in the audience wag.

Spencer pursues the narrative. "Where did I understand you to say you moved from the clubhouse?"

"To Jersey City."

The audience stirs with anticipation at this reference to the notorious flight of the Erie directors.

"And you mentioned you were there with Fisk for nine weeks?"

"Yes."

"Did he not support and maintain you during that time?"

"I don't think so, directly. The money, I suppose,

came from the Erie Railway. I went to Jersey on that occasion with the officers of the Erie company, and the railroad paid all the expense."

"Where were you staying in Jersey City?"

"Taylor's Hotel, where I occupied a suite of rooms."

"Did anybody occupy them with you?"

"All the time, do you mean?"

"You know what I mean."

"Mr. Fisk did, sometimes."

"Anybody else?"

"During the day it was used as a sort of rendezvous by the officers."

"During the night only by yourself and Colonel Fisk?"

"Yes."

Spencer lets this picture—of Josie and Fisk on the lam in Taylor's Hotel—sink in. He then asks for details about the stock operations from which Josie received her income. "Did you see any of them?"

"It was not necessary for me to see them personally."

"Then the money you supposed came from these operations came to you from Fisk personally?"

"Yes."

Spencer asks about Josie's house. "You changed your residence to your present dwelling at what time?"

"1868, I think."

"Where did you get the means to purchase the house?"

"Out of my stock speculations."

"And through the same process and in the same way you describe?"

"Not exactly."

"What was the difference?"

"From the money I made out of the stock speculations I bought government bonds and held these some
time."

"Who got these bonds?"

"I think Mr. Fisk's clerk bought them for me."

"Who furnished money to buy these bonds?"

"It was furnished out of these stock speculations."

"Did you get the money personally and give it for these
bonds, or did not Mr. Fisk furnish all these moneys?"

"He did not. I held the money given for the bonds in
my hands before the bonds were bought."

"Where did you get that money?"

"From Fisk."

Spencer nods as if to underline these words: "From
Fisk." He consults his papers. He walks across the courtroom and back.

He asks about the letters Fisk has written her. Did she
ever give the letters to anyone else?

"I never did."

"Did you supply them to Mr. Stokes?"

The audience buzzes. Josie realizes she has stumbled.
She answers slowly: "I gave them to him, to the number
of about seventy-five."

"They were the original letters that Colonel Fisk had
written to you during your intimacy with him?"

"Yes."

"And you gave them to Mr. Stokes for what purpose?"

"Because he told me it would benefit him in the case that was pending between him and Mr. Fisk at the time."

"You furnished these letters to Mr. Stokes at his request, he saying to you that they would be a benefit to him in this litigation?"

"I did." She doesn't like how this sounds. "I did not mean it would be a benefit so much as an explanation."

"Did he ever return them to you?"

"No, to my surprise."

"Have you seen any of these letters since?"

"Never."

"You don't personally know what became of them?"

"Not personally."

"Did you furnish these letters to any person in the employ of the *Herald* office?"

"Never."

"You furnished them to Mr. Stokes?"

"Yes."

"To be used against Fisk?"

"Yes."

Another pause from Spencer, to let the court, the jury, and the audience appreciate the implications for blackmail of this admission.

Spencer brings Bill Tweed and Tammany Hall into the conversation. "Did you go to Albany about the matter?" he asks Josie.

"Yes."

"To whom?"

"To Mr. Tweed."

For what purpose?

"I thought there would be a good deal of publicity about this matter, and I wanted to avoid it."

It has been a long session, but the injection of Tweed into the tale ends it with a wicked twist, one that is potentially damning to Josie. Spencer sits down and lets all present ponder Josie's shameless treachery in working her feminine wiles on Tweed to further her blackmail scheme against Tweed's friend and ally and her erstwhile lover, Jim Fisk.

15

Josie's testimony in the libel trial is carried in all the papers; from Thanksgiving Day till Christmas it drives the gossip mills of New York City and across the state. The personal aspect of the scandal is reason enough for New Yorkers to pay attention; rarely do the rich and powerful find themselves so exposed as Fisk has become in this messy love triangle. "On the one side is Colonel Fisk, Prince of Erie, owner of the Grand Opera House, Lord of the Isles, famed in love and war," the *Herald* mocks. "On the other the Cleopatra of the period, who has worked as much mischief in her own way with the unfortunate Fisk as did the Egyptian goddess of love and sensuality on the luckless Antony."

But the political potential of the scandal is equally enticing. The involvement of Tweed makes the Fisk-Mansfield-Stokes affair politically explosive. Tweed's cumulative missteps have weakened him; bettors lay odds that new sins discovered in the libel case will bring him and Tammany down.

Judge Bixby promises that justice will be swift in his Yorkville court. "If the lawyers in this case think they are going to make a long winter's job of it, they are mistaken," he declares in early December. "I will take up the case and carry it on day after day until it is concluded. I will not allow myself to be checkmated by the lawyers in carrying out this resolve."

But he can't control the calendar completely, and the new year arrives before the court resumes its hearings. January 6, 1872, is bitterly cold in Manhattan, and the courtroom is hardly warmer. The custodians have taken this Saturday morning off, and the coal stove in the center of the room has not been lit. The judge allows the counsel and witnesses to keep their coats on and does so himself.

Marietta Williams again accompanies Josie. This time Ned Stokes appears, too, although he arrives separately from Josie. Every eye in the courtroom follows him as he walks to his seat, for this is the man who has stolen Josie from Fisk and set the entire sordid spectacle in motion. Fisk has learned at the last minute that Stokes is coming; he can't bring himself to be in the same room as his rival and stays away.

Josie enters the witness stand again. Fisk's counsel Beach inquires how she met Fisk. "Are you acquainted with Miss Annie Wood?" he asks.

"Yes, I formed her acquaintance about six years ago in Washington."

"Did you have a conversation with her in relation to Mr. Fisk?"

"No."

"Did you ask Miss Wood to introduce you to Mr. Fisk after she had given you a description of him and of his character?"

"No. I met him accidentally at her house."

"Do you recollect on that occasion pointing to your dress and saying in substance that was the best you had in the world, and you had not money enough to pay your week's rent?"

"I don't remember anything of the kind."

"Did you say to her that you wanted to know him, as you had no way of earning your living?"

"I have no recollection of anything of the kind. I never said to Miss Wood, before or after my introduction to Fisk, that I was poor and needy, because I was not in such a condition."

"Did you later tell Miss Wood that Mr. Fisk had taken a fancy to you, but that he had not done much for you yet?"

"I never told her so."

Referring to a subsequent incident, Beach demands: "Did you show Miss Wood some costly diamonds and elegant dresses which you said were given you by Fisk?"

"No."

Josie's attorney McKeon objects that these questions have been fed to Beach by someone with a "wicked heart" and an intent to "insult the witness."

Beach responds: "I am not able to judge of the character and heart of the gentleman who furnished me these questions. But I may be permitted to say they don't come from Mr. Fisk."

"I suppose they come from someone who is ready to do his dirty work," McKeon answers.

Judge Bixby sustains the objection.

Beach pushes forward nonetheless. "Did you say, 'There, Annie, look at these compared with my stock when I got acquainted with Fisk. Then I had nothing but that black and white silk dress, and no money in my purse and owing some rent'?"

McKeon objects again. Judge Bixby again excludes the question.

"Did Miss Wood reply to that, 'You have been with him long enough to have got more than that if you were smart'? And did you answer you did not mean to beat him too fast?"

Another objection, again sustained.

"Did Miss Wood ask you upon that occasion if you esteemed or loved Mr. Fisk, and did you reply: 'No, I don't love him, only his money. He is not the style of man I like. I will get all the money I can out of him and then he may go'?"

McKeon jumps to his feet. This interrogation is all for

the newspapers, he declares: to create a sensation and distract from the case at hand. Judge Bixby sustains the objection.

Beach alters his course. "Do you know Nelly Peris?"

"Yes, I did. I sent for her to my house in Twenty-third Street. She might have been there when Mr. Stokes was present."

"Do you recollect that you three were talking upon any occasion when you had a conversation in regard to making money out of Fisk?"

"Never. I did not say in words or substance that I intended to blackmail him."

Josie has been calm until now, but suddenly she struggles with her emotions and breaks down. She apologizes to the court and says she feels ill.

Judge Bixby comes to her aid. He comforts her verbally and glowers at Beach, who terminates the questioning.

Josie steps down and, still crying, leaves the courtroom.

16

The spectators in the Yorkville court appreciate what the rest of New York will learn when the next day's papers hit the newsstands: that the Fisk team has impeached Josie Mansfield's testimony, impugned her motives, and caused her to flee the courtroom—but not caused her to recant her story.

It is now her alleged accomplice's turn to enter the witness box. Stokes's debonair nonchalance contrasts utterly with the sobbing disconcertion of Josie; he treats his testimony as a mildly amusing diversion from what a handsome young man ought to be doing on a Saturday.

The hostile tone of Beach's questions affects Stokes not at all. He recounts his background and his relationship to Josie. "I am thirty years of age," he says, "and have resided at the Hoffman House since last July. I am married and have a family. I first formed the acquaintance of Miss Mansfield in Philadelphia some three years ago; I

was there on business and met her accidentally. I had a
friend with me at the time, but I had rather not answer
his name. I first visited Miss Mansfield at her house in
this city when Mr. Fisk took me there to dine. I don't
remember the date, but I think it was about two years
ago. She then resided in the house she now occupies. I
have called on her, but how frequently I cannot say. I
cannot form a correct idea how often I visited her in the
last six months—probably eight or ten times a month. It
may be more or less, but to the best of my judgment that
is about the average. I had no stated times for calling on
her, and had not been in the habit of doing so. I might
have, sometimes, called upon her three or four times a
week, but other weeks I did not see her at all. I cannot
locate a single week when I did not see her. I have gone
in there and dined, but that is the only meal I have taken
there. I did not go to dinner by appointment, but I very
well knew the dinner hour."

The courtroom laughter that follows this final statement throws Beach off. But after letting the good humor
fade he resumes the attack. "Have you threatened unless
Fisk settled that you would pursue and crush him?"

"In a legal way I have said so, but not in a physical
manner."

"Have you threatened to make publications in the
newspapers against him again and again?"

"Yes, to expose this case and the manner in which he
has swindled me."

"Have you not made propositions to settle with him?"

"I have made some propositions in the way of arbitration, but not in any other form, to my knowledge. I said I would take the papers to the legislature and lay them before it in order to injure him."

"When you first visited the house of Miss Mansfield, was Mr. Fisk an habitué of that house?"

"Oh, yes. Mr. Fisk lived there, and Miss Mansfield lived there at the same time. He remained there a year after I commenced to visit her. I do not remember exactly when he was displaced by her. I had nothing to do with it. I took no hand in the direction of the affairs of the house."

"Have you been in the habit of sleeping in that house?"

"Probably not more than three or four times in two years. I have frequently stayed there until ten o'clock in the evening. I hardly ever was in the room alone with Miss Mansfield. Mrs. Williams was generally there."

"You never stayed with Miss Mansfield alone in the room?"

"No, sir."

"You understand the full force of this declaration?"

"Yes. I have no recollection of staying with her alone in the room late in the evening."

"I want you to make the declaration understandingly: I ask you if you have repeatedly and often spent the late hours of the evening alone with Miss Mansfield, alone in the room."

"No, positively. When I remained as late as ten o'clock Mrs. Williams was generally with me."

"Your acquaintance with Miss Mansfield was simply the ordinary acquaintance of a gentleman and a lady?"

"Yes, sir."

"And there was not more familiarity in that house and between you and Miss Mansfield than would be proper and becoming between a married head of a family and Miss Mansfield?"

"There was nothing improper between her and me."

The spectators don't know what to make of this assertion. Many display disbelief that anything not improper could have triggered the storm of emotions that led to the current welter of lawsuits and, just now, to Josie Mansfield's sobbing departure from the courtroom. Of course Stokes would lie, to protect his family if not himself. All eagerly await the testimony of Marietta Williams, to hear if she will confirm Stokes's improbable tale.

17

But they will have to wait. *Judge Bixby keeps his Saturday* sessions short. The court adjourns promptly at two o'clock, and the participants and spectators are turned out into the cold.

Pleased with his performance, Stokes repairs to nearby Delmonico's for a late lunch. He then visits one of his lawyers, Rufus Andrews, who has been monitoring the proceedings of a grand jury Fisk has managed to have convened to consider criminal charges against Stokes for blackmail. Andrews advises Stokes that he has nothing to fear on this front; Fisk's evidence is flimsy, and the grand jury has declined an indictment several times already. Stokes has been contemplating a trip to Providence to defend himself in yet another court action, but he wants to hear from the grand jury before making a final decision about leaving town. Andrews tells him to go to Providence; there will be no indictment. Stokes still worries and so consults Judge Bixby, who likewise dismisses the prospect of an indictment.

Stokes hails a cab and rides downtown to the Hoffman House. He walks up to his room to collect some papers he will need in Providence. He descends to the lobby and discovers a message waiting for him. He reads the message and learns that the grand jury has in fact returned an indictment against him.

This news shatters the good feeling he has carried from the Yorkville court. The tentacles of Fisk, it seems, are everywhere; there is no escaping his malign influence. Perhaps Stokes wonders whether Josie is worth the troubles she has caused him, troubles that will multiply crushingly if the new indictment leads to conviction and prison. Perhaps he wonders if Josie will love him if he is behind bars. Quite possibly he thinks nothing so coherent; in his agitation his thoughts fly this way and that.

He hails a cab and rides to Josie's house. But when he gets there he doesn't go in. He directs the driver around the corner to the Opera House but doesn't go in there either. He has the driver take him down Broadway and gets out near the Grand Central Hotel, between Amity and Bleecker streets.

The Grand Central bills itself as the finest hotel in America, and it is without question the largest, with more than six hundred rooms. In the eighteen months since opening it has become the favored accommodation of well-heeled visitors to New York, and scores of rich residents of the city make it their permanent abode.

Stokes, inwardly still agitated but outwardly calm, enters the hotel and ascends a staircase to the second-floor hallway, which runs north and south, parallel to Broadway. The hotel is moderately busy on this Saturday afternoon, and no one pays this nattily dressed, respectable-looking visitor particular mind. He seems to be waiting for one of the hotel's guests or residents, as several others in the public areas of the hotel are doing. At five minutes past four o'clock Stokes stands at the head of what the hotel calls the ladies' staircase, to distinguish it from the main stairway at the opposite end of the hall.

He is looking down the staircase when Jim Fisk enters it at the bottom. Their eyes meet. Fisk seems surprised, even shocked, to see Stokes. Stokes appears neither surprised nor shocked.

Fisk is more shocked when Stokes produces a pistol. But Fisk doesn't move, perhaps not sure that he is seeing what he is seeing. Stokes fires. The bullet hits Fisk in the abdomen. Stokes fires again. This bullet hits Fisk in the upper arm.

Fisk belatedly turns to escape. He takes a step but stumbles, then falls to the floor.

Stokes leaves him bleeding in the stairwell. He retreats into the second-floor hallway and walks quickly toward the main staircase. Near the head of the stair is the door to the ladies' parlor; he enters and tosses his pistol, a four-shot derringer, on one of the sofas. He returns to the hallway and descends the main stairway, walking even more quickly now, for he hears shouts that a man

91

has been shot in the hotel and the assailant is on the loose. As the shouts grow louder he breaks into a run, causing the proprietor of the hotel, who sees Stokes from behind the main desk, to call to him to stop. The owner yells to the porters to catch him.

Several porters give chase. Stokes dashes down the hallway toward the back doorway to Mercer Street, dodging hotel guests and visitors. He is passing the hotel barbershop, within a few steps of the street, when he loses his footing on the marble floor. He falls awkwardly. He is up again in an instant, but the delay allows the porters to overtake him. They wrestle him to the floor and pin him down. When he ceases to resist, they drag him to the porters' bench at the foot of the grand stairway and hold him for the arrival of the police.

Fisk knows nothing of Stokes's capture. He has staggered to his feet, unaware how seriously he has been wounded. The doorman and other hotel staff assist him up the ladies' staircase to a vacant suite near the head of the stairs. He collapses on the bed, which immediately becomes soaked in his blood. The doorman and the others are puzzled and alarmed at the amount of the blood, for the arm wound—the only one they can see—appears minor. One of the staff rushes to summon medical help. Two physicians, both of them residents of the hotel, arrive within minutes. They order everyone else out of the room and conduct an examination.

They quickly discover the abdominal wound and realize it is by far the more serious. They call for additional help, meanwhile making Fisk as comfortable as possible. His pain isn't great, as shock has set in. He remains conscious, with momentary lapses.

Two more physicians—surgeons—arrive. One probes the wound to locate the bullet and perhaps extract it. But after exploring several inches into Fisk's ample torso, he finds nothing and gives up. The physicians agree that the wound is probably mortal, although they are encouraged when Fisk grows more alert and apparently stronger. They concur that the next hour or two, perhaps a bit longer, will be critical.

The police arrive at the hotel. Stokes is arrested and taken to Fisk's room. The two men face each other: Stokes standing, silent and sullen; Fisk lying on the blood-soaked bed, breathing heavily and with great effort. Stokes looks away from Fisk, trying to avoid his glance. Fisk looks at Stokes but, in his shock, seems bewildered by the whole sequence of events.

All the police want is for Fisk to identify Stokes as his assailant. Fisk does so but says nothing to Stokes. He then falls back on his pillow. Stokes remains silent, neither denying the identification nor affirming it. He is led away.

The police hustle him out of the hotel and along the sidewalk the half block to the Fifteenth Precinct station house on Mercer Street. A growing crowd, attracted by the commotion, trails the police and the prisoner. The captain on duty at the station house tells Stokes he is going to ask him some questions. "You can answer them or not, as you please."

"I will answer nothing," Stokes responds.

"Will you give me your name?"

"Certainly. My name is Edward S. Stokes. I will give you that but nothing more."

He proves as good as his word. The captain orders him placed in a cell.

The police now concentrate on Fisk. Informed by the doctors that Fisk is dying, the captain dispatches the police coroner to take Fisk's antemortem statement, which like other deathbed testimony, is presumptively more reliable than most other statements. Six witnesses, residents of the hotel and the neighborhood, are summoned as a coroner's jury, to corroborate the coroner's record. As they enter Fisk's room they file past Jay Gould and Bill Tweed, who have heard the news and hurried to the hotel. Whether the purpose of Gould and Tweed is to comfort their partner or keep delirium or approaching judgment from loosening his tongue about their shared secrets, they don't say.

Fisk is lying on his back covered with blankets. His wounded arm is outside the covers, elevated to slow the bleeding. His head is propped on pillows.

The coroner begins by asking Fisk's name and residence. Fisk provides them, his voice just above a whisper.

"Do you believe that you are about to die?" the coroner asks. This question must be answered in the affirmative for the testimony to qualify as specially truthful.

"I feel I am in a very critical condition," Fisk answers.

This isn't good enough for the coroner. "Have you any hopes of recovery?" he asks.

"I hope so."

This fails the test, too. Perhaps the coroner appreciates the irony of asking Fisk to abandon hope for life in order to identify the man who has brought about his imminent death. Perhaps, inured to death, the coroner is inured to irony as well. In any event, he proceeds. "Are you willing to make a true statement of the manner in which you received the injuries?"

"I am."

Fisk is sworn and gives his statement. With considerable effort he retraces the events since arriving at the hotel. He says he recognized Stokes at the head of the stairs and saw something in his hand. He says he saw the flash from the pistol muzzle and heard the report of the powder about the same time he felt the first bullet pierce his abdomen. He describes being hit the second time and falling. He remembers being helped to the room and identifying Stokes.

The statement requires less than two minutes. It is shortly transcribed, and Fisk signs it in a shaking hand.

The coroner's jury delivers a succinct report: "That James Fisk, Jr., came to his injuries by pistol-shot wounds, at the hands of Edward S. Stokes, at the Grand Central Hotel, Jan. 6, 1872."

❧ 18 ❧

By this time half of New York, it seems, has heard of the shooting. The crowd continues to grow on the street outside the Grand Central Hotel, with as many as can push past the police finding their way into the lobby. They are intensely curious but in a somber, respectful way. They whisper questions on Fisk's condition and chances; those on the inside relay to the outdoor contingent the updates posted at the foot of the main stairway. Some mutter assessments of Stokes and his motive in the shooting. Night falls, and they maintain their vigil.

Fisk, still in the bedroom of suite 213, drifts in and out of consciousness. At ten o'clock he queries the attending physician: "Doctor, is there an even chance of my getting well again?" When transmitted to those downstairs and outside, the phrasing of Fisk's plea for encouragement is taken as evidence of how hard the speculative, odds-reckoning spirit dies. The doctor replies with comforting assurance; Fisk nods and drifts off again.

Fisk's personal attorney draws up a will. Fisk is roused to sign it; Jay Gould appends his signature as witness. The terms of the will are not formally disclosed, but hotel staff tell friends who tell the press that most of Fisk's money will go to his wife, with some for his sister and father and an endowment for the Ninth Regiment. Gould is named as executor of the will.

At half past four on the morning of Sunday, January 7, Fisk awakens sufficiently to ask how he is doing. The doctor responds, "Nicely." Fisk nods and fades again, this time for several hours as the opiates administered for his postshock pain take effect.

At seven o'clock, as the city is slowly waking to the Christian Sabbath, Mrs. Fisk arrives. She has, till now, ignored the scandal surrounding her husband; she has kept to her house in Boston and avoided the press. But she can't, and won't, ignore her husband in his dying moments. She received the news of the shooting via telegraph and has taken the overnight train. She steps past the shivering vigil keepers as she enters the hotel; they whisper and point as she goes by. She climbs the stairs to her husband's room.

At eight o'clock the physicians who have worked on Fisk gather. They take his vital signs—pulse rate 130, respiration 20—even as he continues to sleep. The pulse is too fast and the breathing too shallow for one so heavily sedated. They post a new bulletin: "Col. Fisk is sinking."

His breathing grows more labored. Mrs. Fisk begins to

sob and then to wail. A friend who has accompanied her from Boston tries to calm her, to little effect.

Fisk's breathing grows fainter. At 10:40 it stops, then comes in spasmodic gasps. At 10:45 it stops again and does not resume. The doctors declare him dead. He is thirty-six years old.

19

Josie is in seclusion in her house on Twenty-third Street.
She learned of the shooting an hour after it occurred,
from a reporter seeking a reaction. Stunned by the news,
she slammed the door in the reporter's face and has
remained behind drawn curtains since.

The silence from her house feeds rumors that she has
fled the city. The rumors sound plausible, considering
her unsettled state in court on the afternoon of the shooting. New Yorkers want to know the whereabouts of the
most notorious woman in their city; the authorities will
certainly wish to question her in connection with the
shooting.

One reporter plants himself at her residence. He sees
nothing: no movement and only the faintest light within.
After a long time he ascends the steps and rings the door-
bell. Nothing happens. The outside door remains bolted;
the hallway is dark. He turns to leave.

But then he hears the bolt being pulled and the door handle turn. A quavering woman's voice asks through the narrow opening: "What do you want, sir?"

He pulls a card from his wallet, identifying him, and scribbles in the corner: "On business." He asks the woman to give the card to Miss Mansfield.

The door closes. He wonders whether to stay or go, and decides to stay. The woman returns after a few minutes. "Unless it is very important," she says, "Miss Mansfield can't see you."

But this time she has opened the door a crack wider. The reporter peers through. By the flicker of a gas lamp opposite the door, he recognizes the woman as Josie Mansfield herself.

The reporter declines to press his luck, not least since he has achieved the principal aim of his surveillance: to discover whether Josie is still in the city. He says he will call again when it is more convenient.

He descends the stairs to Twenty-third Street, walks the several steps to the corner, and turns onto Eighth Avenue. Suddenly a policeman with a grimy shawl around his neck, to ward off the cold, and a dirty mass of red hair hurries across the street and waves his nightstick in the reporter's face. "What was you doing in there?" the officer demands.

"In where?" the reporter says.

"In Miss Mansfield's."

"I was doing nothing in there, because I was not in."

"Didn't I see you with my own eyes, coming out? Come along, you're my prisoner." He grabs the reporter by the shoulder.

"All right," the reporter says, and lets himself be taken to the precinct house on Twentieth Street. There he is charged with coming out of Miss Mansfield's residence.

The reporter denies that he has been in the house, before asking why this should be a crime. He says he can prove he wasn't in the house; Miss Mansfield will be happy to testify to that.

The sergeant on duty sends a second patrolman back to the house, with another of the reporter's cards. In a few minutes the second man returns and says Miss Mansfield has corroborated the reporter's story.

The sergeant takes the reporter aside. He explains that the arresting patrolman is new on the job and perhaps overeager. The police higher-ups have given the order to guard the Mansfield house lest Miss Mansfield try to escape. The patrolman must have thought the reporter was the lady in disguise.

The reporter accepts the sergeant's apology and leaves to file his story.

⚞ 20 ⚟

New York receives the news of Fisk's death with mixed emotions. Horace Greeley lectures Wall Street and America for having produced such a sorry specimen of humanity. "Fiction furnishes few personages more absurd in qualities and in fortune," the *Tribune* editor and self-anointed conscience of liberalism declares. "Even the story of Aladdin ceases to seem so impossible when we think of this illiterate Vermonter stepping almost without an interval from his cart of notions to take the reins of a great corporation, to purchase today a fleet and tomorrow a theater, to make today a panic and tomorrow a statute, to buy legislatures and prima donnas, to dazzle Wall Street with the brilliancy of his thefts and Central Park with the splendor of his equipages. . . . It is not creditable to our society and our civilization that such careers are possible." But Fisk could have done worse, Greeley admits. "He was no hypocrite—if that is any praise. When he devoured the widow's substance, he differed from many of his associates in refraining from the pretense of long prayers. In the household circle where he was known before he became the James Fisk, Jr., of history, he will be sincerely mourned and wept. Perhaps it is as well that we should leave his story as it is known to the world—a warning and a lesson."

Fisk's colleagues and the general public gather at the hotel to see the body, which is placed in an open coffin in the parlor outside the bedroom where he died. Jay Gould, weary from the long night, rests blankly in a chair a few feet from the coffin as mourners file past. "It was a picture never seen before and never to be seen again," an eyewitness records: "the dead Fisk, gazed upon by hundreds, with pity only because of the manner of his death, and the living Gould sitting unmoved beside the corpse, to be looked upon with abhorrence by many who passed, for the deeds which he had wrought with him who was dead."

Just before the coffin is closed, Bill Tweed arrives. He doesn't want to be seen, especially not now. The public reaction to the Orange Day riot emboldened the state's attorney to investigate the activities of Tweed's Tammany ring; indictments are imminent. Tweed judges that the less public fraternizing with Fisk and Gould the better. But he feels sad for Fisk and wants to see his partner in collusion one last time. He waits until everyone else, including Gould, has gone. He slips into the parlor for a moment's view. He follows the coffin as it is carried through the halls of the hotel to the rear entrance on Mercer Street. Only when the wooden box passes out the door does he turn aside and disappear down another hallway.

Fisk's fellow militiamen mourn his passing. "It is with deep regret that the Brigadier-General commanding announces the death of Col. James Fisk, Jr., Ninth Regiment Infantry," his superior proclaims. "His loss will be sincerely felt, and his place in the National Guard not easily filled." Fisk's lieutenant issues an order to the Ninth: "This command will assemble at the armory in full dress uniform (white cross and body belts and white gloves), with crape on the left arm, on Monday, Jan. 8, to pay the last tribute of respect to our lamented Colonel. Assembly at 12 o'clock M."

When that hour arrives, the body is lying in state at the Opera House. The city has turned out in force to bid farewell to the Prince of Erie, to watch the parade that transports the body to the train for Vermont, to see if the Irish and the Orangemen will battle again, to determine whether Tweed will show his face in public.

The parade goes off without a hitch. The Irish tribes leave their shillelaghs at home. Tweed stays away.

The coffin is placed on the train, which pulls out of the station at three. Fisk returns, finally, to his native state.

Jim Fisk

Josie Mansfield

Ned Stokes

Cornelius Vanderbilt

Jay Gould

William Tweed

Wall Street

Vanderbilt and Fisk at work

The Grand Opera House

The Gold Room on Black Friday

"WHAT A FALL WAS THERE, MY COUNTRYMEN!"

The morning after

The Orange Day riot

The Grand Central Hotel

The fatal meeting

Mourning Fisk, after a fashion

The Tombs

21

Ned Stokes, meantime, sleeps soundly in the Tombs. He appears to be at peace with himself, greeting his keepers at the New York City jail with a smile as they deliver breakfast and the morning papers. He ignores the stares of the other inmates, who gawk and point at this gentleman among them. He seems unaware of the two hundred extra policemen mustered by the city to guard his cell against the possible wrath of the Ninth Regiment at the assassination of their beloved patron. His brother brings him collars, cuffs, cravats, and socks from the Hoffman House, so that Stokes may be presentable when his lawyers arrive to discuss his case.

A rumor has circulated—apparently as a result of Stokes having been moved from one cell to another, leaving the first empty—that he has committed suicide. Reporters scramble to confirm or refute. "He persists in living, and living very comfortably," the first with the facts, a *Times* man, explains. "He was taken to cell No. 50, the one assigned to him by Warden Stacom, and which has been handsomely fitted up at the prisoner's expense. It is richly carpeted, the walls are papered and hung with a few fine pictures, and a new hair mattress and new bed-clothing have been substituted for the coarse prison articles. Altogether, the cell now appears more like a young lady's boudoir."

The reporter pays a second visit, arriving just as Stokes returns from a hearing in which his lawyers have unsuccessfully challenged the finding of the coroner's jury, that Stokes's shots killed Fisk. "The prisoner's demeanor after the verdict of the jury was unchanged; indeed, if anything, his spirits were more buoyant. As soon as he left the court room he partook of a hearty dinner." The prisoner's confidence is contagious in the close quarters of the Tombs: "Bets of $100 to $50 were freely offered, yesterday, that Stokes will not be hung."

Stokes remains upbeat days later when a grand jury indicts him for Fisk's murder. Reporters find him standing in the doorway of his cell, leaning against the wall, unlighted cigar in his mouth, whittling a quill toothpick with a penknife. "You newspapermen are all wrong about my case," he tells the group. "When it comes to trial you will see I have one of the strongest cases to present you ever heard of." He smiles winningly, reminding the newsmen what Josie saw in him. "I have no more fears of the result than you have. I am confident I will get out of it. That Erie gang is working against me. It is one of the worst the world ever knew, and the head of it is an astute villain—that little Jay Gould. They seem to have the newspapers, though I don't know how they can secure their influence."

But the trial is delayed. Stokes's lawyers challenge the validity of his indictment, asserting that the grand jury was selected by unconstitutional means. The district attorney's office defends the indictment and the procedure, to preserve its case against Stokes but also to safeguard indictments it has brought by similar means against the Tweed ring. Stokes discovers, with a pained sense of irony, that winning his own case may jeopardize the people's case against Boss Tweed, the facilitator of Fisk's crimes.

The days become weeks, the weeks months, with Stokes still in jail. His spirits sag and his patience grows thin. The papers reveal that he is losing—perhaps has lost—the battle for public opinion. Fisk is remembered with increasing fondness, his financial manipulations now seen as a natural part of the Wall Street game. Stokes is cast as a woman stealer, a blackmailer, a cold-blooded murderer.

Stokes's patience snaps when he learns of a play being performed at Niblo's Garden, called *Black Friday,* which recounts the gold conspiracy and concludes with the shooting at the Grand Central Hotel. He has been silent about his case until now, at his lawyers' insistence, but he can keep quiet no longer. He releases a letter "To the Public," in which he recounts his travails. "I have suffered physically from unnecessarily close confinement," he says. "I have suffered more mentally from the repeated and gross misrepresentations in newspapers under the control and influence of my enemies." He has heard and read the continued allegations that he conspired with Josie Mansfield to extort money from Fisk. "These accusations are unqualifiedly false." His relations with Miss Mansfield were merely those of a friend, he insists again.

He is outraged that Fisk's associates are portraying the deceased as the aggrieved party in his dealings with Stokes; the truth, Stokes swears, is entirely the opposite. "I have been in legitimate business for the past ten years. With the exception of a reverse in 1865, I had been generally successful until I was induced to take James Fisk, Jr., as partner in my oil business in Brooklyn." Fisk soon showed his real character as a swindler and a thug. "By him I was flagrantly robbed and outraged. My refinery was seized at midnight on Sunday by a lawless gang of ruffians, without any process of law, while I was thrown into prison and thereby enjoined from even attempting to proceed to regain my own property." Litigation eventually yielded a marginally acceptable settlement, but an unscrupulous Erie lawyer and a crooked Tammany judge deprived him even of this.

The production at Niblo's includes the most egregious falsehoods yet, Stokes says: "The incidents of this libelous play require no denial with them who know me, but 3,000 persons who know nothing of my antecedents or character nightly witness this misrepresentation of me as a gambler, a roué, forger and assassin, and possibly may accept it for truth." The characterization is monstrously absurd from start to finish. "No man can honestly assert that I knowingly ever wronged anyone, and as for being an adept at cards, I barely know one card from another." The forgery charge is equally ludicrous; Stokes says he knows nothing about the insidious practice.

As for being an assassin, he will rebut that allegation in court. "When all the facts of this unfortunate affair are developed, and when it shall be proved how infamously the witnesses perjured themselves at the coroner's inquest, then public opinion, which has been based upon false statements, will set in my favor. I am anxious, and always have been anxious, for a speedy trial by an honest jury of my fellow men."

22

Stokes's trial comes, but not speedily. The summer of 1872 has almost reached New York by the time the murder trial begins, in the New York Court of Oyer and Terminer. Defendants in Judge D. P. Ingraham's court are rarely as well represented as Ned Stokes is today, and the prosecutors never deploy more legal firepower than the district attorney now does against Stokes. Indeed, John McKeon, heading the Stokes side, immediately questions the presence of William Beach, Fisk's lawyer in Josie's libel suit, and William Fullerton, his associate, at the side of District Attorney Samuel Garvin. "These gentlemen now employed have the gold of private individuals in their pockets," McKeon declares. "These gentlemen were hired for the purpose of producing a conviction." He looks at Beach and Fullerton and then at his client. "It is a terrible spectacle to see private counsel arranging themselves on the side of the prosecution, and with blood-hound perseverance hound this man." Judge Ingraham accepts McKeon's question and says he'll rule on it tomorrow. For now Beach and Fullerton stay.

The examination of prospective jurors commences promisingly. Myer Homburger, who identifies himself as a merchant and importer, says that he has never had any business dealings with Messrs. Fisk, Gould, or Tweed; has never held a paid position with the Erie Railroad or the City of New York; has read various accounts of the shooting but has formed no opinion in the matter; does not remember reading of any particular expressions uttered by Mr. Fisk just before his death; has a general impression that Mr. Stokes shot Mr. Fisk but if placed on the jury would have no bias against the prisoner and would render a verdict based entirely on the evidence adduced in the trial. Myer Homburger is accepted as a juror.

But things soon slow down. William Russell, hardware dealer, is rejected for having done business with the Opera House. Louis Slocum, oculist, admits to having an opinion that will be hard to alter and is rejected. Jacob Davidson, shoe dealer, professes scruples about the death penalty and is rejected.

Then Roderick Hogan, hatter, though having gained an initial impression regarding the guilt of the defendant, says he has modified this impression lately and will have no difficulty rendering a decision based on the evidence. Hatter Hogan is accepted and sworn in.

The two jurors turn out to be the day's total yield. Judge Ingraham orders them sequestered and rules that the fifteen persons who failed to answer the jury summons will be fined one hundred dollars each.

On the morning of the second day, Ingraham delivers his decision that Beach and Fullerton will be allowed to assist the prosecution. He doesn't require them to reveal who is compensating them, and they don't volunteer. But the unrebutted assumption is that they are in the pay of Jay Gould, Bill Tweed, or both. Beach, however, remarks that previously he has represented Stokes. "During some two years when I have acted as his counsel, and knew him in social life, there never has been the least unpleasantness between us, and not for a single moment have I entertained a single sentiment of hostility against him." He turns to Stokes, smiles, and says, "That is right, Ed, is it not?" Stokes grimaces but nods.

Completing the jury takes several more days. One man is rejected for knowing Tweed, another for having made a wager on whether Stokes will hang (he doesn't say which way he bet), a third for residing in New Jersey (how he received a summons is unclear), a fourth for not being a citizen, a fifth for having enjoyed the play *Black Friday*, and dozens, then scores, and finally hundreds of others for similar reasons. Judge Ingraham gets testy. "No man except a fool could read newspaper accounts of the shooting and not form an opinion on the subject," he says, after the defense cites such opinion, for perhaps the

150th time, as grounds for rejection. "If he could, he would have no mind at all." The judge tells the two sides to get serious, and after one further day of procrastination, during which not a single juror is accepted from a hundred prospects, the twelfth juror is at last impaneled.

District Attorney Garvin opens for the prosecution. The essence of the case is premeditation, he tells the court and the jury. "The law is that if the life of Colonel Fisk was taken by design and premeditation with intent so to do at the time when the transaction took place, then the prisoner is guilty of murder in the first degree, and you are bound so to find. There are no refinements about this case, no doubts about the question involved, no trouble surrounding it. It is a plain straightforward case, either one way or the other, and you will have no trouble coming to a conclusion."

He lays out the people's case. "We shall prove that about four o'clock on the afternoon of the 6th of January, 1872, the prisoner was on Broadway, nearly opposite his hotel. Next the prisoner was seen passing the Grand Opera House a few minutes thereafter. As he passed he looked directly into the window where Colonel Fisk stood. In a very short period of time subsequently he was seen again in Broadway, above the Grand Central Hotel. He was seen to enter that hotel in a hurry, go up the stairway, stand at the head of the stairs, laying in wait and watching as if for the appearance of someone who, at that time, nobody but the spirit who sits before you today knew. Not less than five minutes afterward Colonel Fisk stepped out of his carriage and walked up that stairway. At the head of the stairs stood the accused, pistol in hand. He fired the first and mortal wound upon Colonel Fisk. Then to make sure, he fired a second shot. The first shot was embedded in his bowels, and he died the following day.

"Now, gentlemen, if that is true, if these facts are proven in evidence, if he did lie in wait for Colonel Fisk and shot, and that was a mortal wound, and he died, I shall ask you, as good men, to render a verdict of premeditated murder against this prisoner, and let him take the consequences of his crime. If, on the other hand, there is any evidence produced by him which relieves him from this responsibility, then it will be for you to listen to him, hear it, give it such consideration as it shall be entitled to, and, if he is not guilty, so pronounce and let him go free. If, again, it turns out that the evidence we present is true, then under all the considerations which operate upon man, you are bound to pronounce him guilty and let the law of God and man take its course."

 **23**

Garvin's dramatic statement catches New York off guard, coming as it does at the end of seven dreary days of jury selection, during which the city's attention has wandered. But in signaling that the real business of the trial is beginning, it revives interest in the case. The next day a huge crowd clamors to enter the courtroom. A brigade of police and a special posse of citizens summoned by Judge Ingraham are required to keep order on the street outside the court and to make sure that room is saved inside for those conducting the trial.

A rail separates the principals and the jury from the lucky members of the general public who manage to gain admittance. Ned Stokes's father and brother have come. So have several mysterious, or at any rate unidentified, young ladies who appear to have a special interest in the case. Do they know Stokes? Personally? Others in the audience point at them and whisper.

The background buzzing diminishes as counsel Beach and Fullerton enter, escorting two women wearing black dresses and full veils over their faces. From their apparel, sobs, and general demeanor the audience surmises that these are the widow of the victim and her friend from Boston. Someone suggests that one or both of the women will testify; the audience quietly but emphatically debates the likelihood of such an event.

Ned Stokes enters, immediately shifting the undercurrent of conversation in a different direction. He tries to appear unconcerned but has difficulty carrying it off. He has visibly aged since last seen in public, on the day of the murder; his black hair is streaked with silver, his face is drawn and pale, his eye lacks its former luster. He seems fully aware of the gravity of his situation: that this trial is for his life.

Judge Ingraham scowls as he takes the bench. He glares at the audience to warn against any outbursts of emotion. He frowns at the opposing legal teams to let the district attorney and the high-priced counsel know that this is *his* court, where *his* rules apply.

The prosecution calls its first witness. Charles Hill identifies himself as a lumber dealer in West Troy who travels to New York frequently on business. He was a guest at the Grand Central Hotel on January 6. "I went into the hotel a little before four o'clock and went up to the second floor by the front elevator," he says. "While standing there I heard the report of a pistol. First I could not say exactly where it proceeded from, but a second followed in quick succession, and appeared to come from the hall on the second side of the elevator. I went to the other side and saw a man standing on the left of the hall; I saw that man make a motion of his hand, turn and come toward me; as he passed I asked what was up and he said there was a man shot. I went on to the stairs and saw a man whom I recognized as Colonel Fisk down, I think, upon the platform of the stairs, leaning on the rail. At that instant someone said, 'There is the man that shot him,' and I immediately followed after him. I returned and went down toward the main stairs until I got to the third step, when they were bringing back this man whom I first saw."

District Attorney Garvin asks, "Who was that man?"

"The prisoner who sits looking at me now," Hill answers.

Under cross-examination by defense counsel McKeon, Hill says he left New York City later on the day of the shooting without speaking to police. "I cannot explain how they knew I had information on the subject. I did not tell it to Mr. Crockett"—of the hotel staff—"because I did not think it best, as I would be detained as a witness."

"You had reason to know a homicide was committed," McKeon demands, "and you did not think it your duty to communicate it to anyone?"

"I thought there was sufficient evidence without it," Hill replies. "I have been here three times since January, and have never communicated to anyone a word of what I knew on this subject. I can't conceive how it leaked out."

The audience ponders who the leaker might be as the second witness takes the stand. Francis Curtis of Roxbury, Massachusetts, was also a guest at the hotel. He says he saw Fisk on the stairs after he was shot and was one of those who helped get Fisk into the suite where he was examined by the doctors. He was present when the police brought the prisoner in. Prosecutor Garvin instructs: "State what the officer said to Colonel Fisk, in the presence of the prisoner."

The defense objects: "Hearsay and incompetent."

Judge Ingraham overrules the objection.

Curtis answers: "The officer asked Colonel Fisk, 'Is that the man?' or 'Do you recognize the man?'—I could not be certain which. Fisk said, 'Yes, that is the man; take him out, take him away.' "

Cross-examining, McKeon asks how Curtis recognized Fisk.

"I had known Fisk for two years," Curtis says. "I saw him aboard the boat, the *Narragansett*"—one of Fisk's steamers. "I afterward saw him in Boston when he was on parade, saw him on his horse." Under further questioning, Curtis describes helping undress Fisk after the shooting. "Colonel Fisk had a cloak or a cape on his shoulder, of a dark color. I took his coat off; I then took out my knife and cut off the sleeve of his shirt, clear above the wound, and either myself or someone bound it with a handkerchief. Colonel Fisk was put to bed; his pants were drawn down over his hips so the wound could be got at; the wound was below the navel, a little to the left of the navel."

The third witness, Peter Coughlin, born in Ireland, is a coal porter at the Grand Central Hotel. He has been called to confirm Stokes's identity and to locate him at the time of the shooting. "He had on a white coat with black collar. I saw him at the head of the stairs. His right hand was in his pocket, the other resting at the head of the stairs." Under cross-examination Coughlin admits he was in the coal closet when the shots were fired; he didn't see them but came out afterward.

John Chamberlain is a resident of New York City who was at the Erie office on the afternoon of January 6. "What part of the building were you in?" the district attorney asks.

"Mr. Fisk's office."

"Did you see the prisoner that afternoon?"

"Yes, sir."

"Where?"

"Saw him about half past three at the corner of Eighth Avenue and Twenty-third Street, going across Eighth Avenue in a coupé."

"Did he have a driver?"

"Yes, sir."

"Did you notice whether he was looking out?"

"He was looking up at the windows of the Erie Railway office."

"State which way they were driving."

"He was just crossing Eighth Avenue, going toward North River, down Twenty-third Street."

"Did you see him after that on that day?"

"No, sir."

"Was Colonel Fisk in the room with you at that time?"

"Yes, sir."

"How long after that did you leave?"

"He soon went down to the Opera House, and I went away."

"Did you see Colonel Fisk after that?"

"I saw him at the Grand Central Hotel."

McKeon cross-examines. "What is your business?" he asks Chamberlain.

"Speculator."

"In what?"

"Everything, nearly."

"What do you speculate in generally?"

"Stocks."

"Ever speculate in stocks with Mr. Fisk?"

"Not in connection with him."

"Have you been operating in the same stocks that he did?"

"Yes, sir, I think I have."

"Were you in the operations of Black Friday?"

"No, sir, I was not in town then."

"You had no puts or calls?"

"I had no puts or calls, but I had some stock, and lost a great deal of money."

"Have you carried on any business at No. 8 Twenty-fifth Street?"

"Yes, sir."

"What?"

"Clubhouse."

"What kind of a clubhouse?"

Chamberlain hesitates. "Gentlemen play cards there."

"For money?"

"Yes, sir."

"Is there such a thing as a faro bank there?"

Chamberlain is slow to answer, perhaps weighing the cost of confessing to illegal gambling against the price of perjury.

McKeon turns to Judge Ingraham. "He is obliged to answer, unless it connects him with some criminal offense," he says. "I suppose the court will instruct him on that point."

The judge puts the question to the witness, who still refuses to answer.

McKeon, having made his point—that Chamberlain is no cherub—moves on. "Were you in the habit of frequently going to the Opera House?"

"Yes, sir, two or three times a week."

"Had you business with the Opera House?"

"Not at all."

"Was it business with Fisk or Gould?"

"Not with Mr. Gould. It was with Mr. Fisk."

"What was the nature of that business?"

"Stock operations."

"How high is Fisk's room from the walk?"

"Second story."

"Pretty high up, is it not?"

"Yes."

"Was Fisk there when you went in?"

"Yes, sir."

"Were you standing near the window?"

"I did stand near the window part of the time, and sat down part of the time."

"Was it not cold weather?"

"Yes, sir."

"Were you not sitting near the fire?"

The audience perks up at this effort to shake the testimony of the witness.

"There was no fire," Chamberlain answers. "It is heated by heaters."

The audience laughs. McKeon frowns. Judge Ingraham pounds his gavel. The witness is excused.

Thomas Hart, twenty, a doorman of the Grand Central Hotel, is the next to testify. The district attorney asks: "Had you seen Stokes in the hotel at any time before you saw Colonel Fisk come in that day?"

"Not before, but afterward. I was cleaning the windows at the foot of the private stairs, at the ladies' entrance."

"Was there any light?"

"Yes, sir, gas lights at the head of the stairs. I took a globe upstairs to clean it, and on looking down I saw

Colonel Fisk come across the sidewalk and come in at the door. He said something to the other boy, and then started to come upstairs with his right hand on the railing. On looking around I saw Stokes come out of the parlor No. 207, and walk along the north side of the hall in a crouched manner, walking light. When he got near to the head of the stairs he stopped and looked down, and then turning round I heard him say, 'I have got to do it now,' or something to that effect. He then walked up to the head of the stairs, and I saw him put up his right hand, resting it on the railing, and I heard two reports of a pistol. I then laid down the globe and went up to within five or six feet of where Stokes was standing. At the first shot I saw Fisk stagger, and at the second he threw up his hands and exclaimed, 'Oh! Oh! Oh, don't!' and slid downstairs. Stokes looked at him, and I saw him make a motion as if putting something under his coat. Turning round, he said, 'There has been a man shot there, and somebody had better come and pick him up and see to him.' I said, 'Yes, and you are the man that shot him.' He made no reply but, turning round, walked quickly toward the first parlor, No. 207, and I saw him make a motion with his right hand as if throwing something away. He then walked quickly toward the main staircase and ran down, and I followed him. When he got downstairs, he said to a man that someone had been shot upstairs and somebody had better go and pick him up. I said, 'Yes, and there goes the man who shot him.' "

The prosecution brings forward several more witnesses. John Redmond was the hall boy at the Grand Central Hotel on January 6; he corroborates Tommy Hart's account of the shooting. Frank Crockett, the front office clerk, describes Stokes running down the stairs and trying to escape out the Mercer Street door. Henry de Carley, a parlor attendant, explains how a lady guest found a pistol—"a very nice pistol, too," de Carley says— in a second-floor parlor.

Dr. James Wood, one of the surgeons called to the scene, testifies as to his examination of Fisk. He describes probing the abdominal wound, unsuccessfully, for the bullet. He explains that the bullet pierced the small intestine in four places, passing in and out of two loops in the intestine, and pierced the colon twice.

The district attorney asks him to state the cause of death.

Wood answers that either shock or inflammation could produce death after such wounds. "But there was not enough of inflammation in this case."

"Then it must be shock?"

"I can account for the death in no other way."

 **24**

Things aren't looking good for Stokes by the time the prose-
cution concludes its argument. The fact of the shooting is
irrefutable and the death of Fisk undeniable. The spectators, nodding assent at the prosecution's key points,
seem convinced; if the jury is a fair sampling of the same
population pool, the gallows must loom large over the
prisoner.

Against the unfavorable mood, John McKeon rises to
speak for the defense. "Gentlemen of the jury," he says,
"this is one of the most important and impressive duties
in which I have ever been engaged." The life of one man
has been cut short; the life of another hangs in the bal-
ance. The jury's duty is to deliver justice to both.

He takes up a document. "Edward S. Stokes is indicted
for what?" he says. "He is indicted in the paper which I
hold in my hand for having on the 6th of January 1872
inflicted a wound on James Fisk, the younger, from

which wound Fisk died." More specifically, the inflicting is alleged to have been done "with malice aforethought" and with "the premeditated design to effect the death" of Fisk.

McKeon explains that he will refute the charge of premeditation, and he begins by asking the jury to consider the deceased. "Mr. Fisk was no ordinary man. I am not one of those who intend to underrate his abilities. He was a man who made the impress of himself on the age in which he lived. Fisk during his lifetime did things which attracted attention not only on this continent but on the other side of the Atlantic." McKeon recounts Fisk's childhood and youth in Vermont, and his migration to Boston for business. "The war raged between the North and the South, and Mr. Fisk, not being governed by any feeling of over-loyalty, went into operations in Confederate cotton and amassed a large sum of money." He moved to New York and began a series of bold speculations. He conspired in the manipulation of the Erie Railroad and in the Black Friday gold raid. The violence of the gold panic surprised even its instigator. "Fisk became alarmed, and from that time forward always went armed." His sponsorship of the Ninth Regiment was characteristically self-interested. "He wanted men of the roughs whom he could use. He pursued a system of brigandage, and his brigands were encamped in the very heart of the city." He threatened those who stood in his way. "Mr. Fisk's common remark was, 'If anyone interferes with us, we never will prosecute him,' and a favorite expression of his was, 'Our touch is cold and clammy.' Another favorite expression was, 'We have graveyards for our friends.' "

Such was the man Edward Stokes shot. "We will show you that this gentleman"—Stokes—"who fired this ball at him made himself obnoxious to Mr. Fisk at a certain time; that he found himself followed from time to time." McKeon describes Fisk's treatment of Dorman Eaton, a civic reformer who challenged favors Fisk had received from Tammany Hall. One night Eaton was returning home after work. "He heard a whistle and saw a man on one side of the street watching him, and another man just near his house; he heard a low whistle, and a moment afterward he was struck down within a hundred feet of Fifth Avenue, and was left there without any sign of life."

The spectators whisper and shift in their seats. Most have heard allegations that Fisk's men sometimes played hard, but New York is a hard town. Yet the brutal assault on Eaton, who barely survived the attack, pushes the boundary even for Fisk and New York. Some in the audience register concern; others seem pleased at the thought of a newly shocking twist in the already sordid tale.

"We will show you that Mr. Fisk organized that," McKeon continues, of the assault. "And we will show you that this man Stokes was told that he would be treated in the same way."

McKeon injects a personal note into his description of Fisk's malignance. "I have lived through the offices of district attorney, for both the state and the United States, for nearly four years. My business as such required me to prosecute perjurers, murderers, slave traders and all of that character. And there never lived a man of whom I was afraid, nor ever met a man who I thought would do me a wrong, until James Fisk, Jr., and I faced each other."

McKeon has a reputation in New York for dauntlessness; this grim assertion provokes chin stroking and head wagging around the courtroom. He extends the moment for maximum effect, discreetly glancing at the audience every few seconds to assess the damage he has done to the prosecution.

He moves on. He recites some of Stokes's history with Fisk. Stokes was managing the family oil refinery when he received a message that Fisk wanted to meet with him. "He was brought over and introduced to him at the Opera House. Fisk said he wanted to get hold of this oil refinery, and if Stokes would manage to keep the rent down he thought he could make a good thing out of it, and he then entered into a plan that every barrel of oil that passed over the road should be charged to every other man engaged in the business, and at the end of the month a drawback train would lay up at the rate of sixty-five cents a barrel. The consequence was there was an immense profit made that yielded something over one hundred thousand dollars a year. This was all taken out of the Erie Railroad Company."

A few in the audience know that these secret kickbacks occur with some regularity at the intersection of the oil and railroad businesses. But to hear that Fisk was so egregiously robbing his own company nonetheless causes a rustling in the courtroom.

McKeon again pauses for effect. He shuffles his papers and stares at the ceiling. Then he plunges into the part of the story everyone in the room has been waiting for. "I introduce to you the name of a person of whom you have heard a great deal. Stokes was introduced to Miss Mansfield in November 1869, at the Continental Hotel in Philadelphia." The person arranging the introduction was an agent of Fisk's, McKeon says. "The first time that Stokes ever saw Miss Mansfield at her house, he called upon her on New Year's Day, and was invited by Fisk to dine with him there. He did dine with him." Jay Gould was also present, as were several officials of New York City and State.

It was shortly after this that Miss Mansfield grew disenchanted with Fisk. "She turned him away, would have nothing to do with him. For what? It is enough to know that Mr. Fisk had a wife living in Boston, where she remained while he lived here with Miss Mansfield. Now, I want you to mark the point that she became disgusted with him—disgusted as any woman ought to be, for a number of reasons. But the reason that she left him was that her health required that she should drive him away; that it was necessary that she should have nothing to do with him, and she separated herself from him." McKeon doesn't explain the nature of Josie's health problems, perhaps presuming that delicacy will prevent the prosecution from inquiring. He does say that Fisk refused to let her alone. "Fisk was so infatuated with this woman that he begged her to take him back, and she, having the weakness of a woman, yielded to Fisk's entreaties."

During this same period Fisk sought to revise his kickback understanding with Stokes—to Fisk's benefit, naturally. Stokes resisted, whereupon Fisk threw the full power of the Erie and of his political influence against him. "Stokes's business was paralyzed." Facing ruin, Stokes appealed to Fisk for mercy. "Stokes was on his knees to him." Fisk arranged a late-night meeting at Josie Mansfield's house. "This woman possesses an abundance of intelligence," McKeon says, in a meaningful aside, "for which, notwithstanding her surrounding circumstances, she ought to be credited. A woman of twenty-four years of age—in all my conversations with her I have never seen her superior." Fisk tried to intimidate Stokes. "He said his powers were so great there was no resisting him; that through his political associates in this city and through the political ring"—the Tweed ring— "his power was such over judges and all public officers that they were completely under his control, and that they were ruling this city with a rod of iron; and that the Protestants never ruled France more severely than they were ruling New York at that time."

But Fisk had an additional demand, one more personal. It involved Josie Mansfield, McKeon says. He quotes Fisk: "I want you to get back her affection for me." Stokes responded, "I have no control of that. I will have nothing to do with it."

Fisk was outraged. "He vowed vengeance against Stokes," McKeon says. "It was a feeling of jealousy, a feeling of revenge which prompted him from time to time to endeavor to gain control of Stokes for the purpose of getting Miss Mansfield back again into his affections."

Fisk made Stokes's life a living hell, McKeon says. "Stokes was told that he had better arm and protect himself—that Fisk would take his life." Stokes grew terrified. "We will show that men were following him night and day—that he could not go out even in a public place like Broadway that he would not be followed from place to place and the attention of persons called to that fact. The poor fellow was so anxious for this settlement that his mind became disturbed."

Yet Fisk only intensified the pressure on Stokes, McKeon says. Fisk sent a gang of toughs to seize the refinery by force. He orchestrated an indictment of Stokes on an embezzlement charge and had him locked up in the Mulberry Street jail. He rigged the arbitration of the oil dispute so that Stokes received a mere pittance. He bribed the houseboy of Miss Mansfield to swear that she and Stokes were plotting to blackmail Fisk. "He was a willing tool," McKeon says of the boy. "As soon as the boy had made these statements, he disappeared from the state of New York; if he had not, he would have been arrested for perjury. After the Yorkville court saw through Fisk's machinations and neutralized them, he engineered another indictment in another court, which indictment was handed down on January 6."

This pushed Stokes to the edge of insanity. Yet far from seeking Fisk out, he tried to avoid him. The merest chance took him to the Grand Central Hotel that afternoon. "At four o'clock he crossed over the street on the corner of Broadway and Great Jones," McKeon says. "Just then he was met by a gentleman of respectability and standing, who left a stage and said, 'Ned, what are you about? Come along with me; I am going to Niblo's to get tickets for *The Black Crook*.' They walked down together, and as they passed the Grand Central he thought he saw a lady in the hotel bowing to him, and he said to this gentleman, 'I think there is a lady I met in Saratoga; come along over with me.' The gentleman excused himself, and Stokes left him and went across to the ladies' entrance. Then he saw that he did not know her, and walked through the main hall toward the stairs. The lady passed him here and went upstairs. He had his pistol in his pocket, being in fear for his life, as I have said. As he came to the turn, and got to the head of the stairs, he looked down and saw Fisk coming in at the bottom of the stairs. His first feeling was to go down, and as he did so he saw Fisk draw his pistol, and then he pulled his pistol and fired twice."

The audience members gasp and stare at one another in surprise. This is the first time anyone at the trial has suggested that Fisk had a pistol. They shift forward in their seats to hear McKeon's corollary to this amazing assertion.

"When Stokes fired he was in imminent danger of his life," the defense attorney declares. "If he hadn't drawn, this man would have shot him dead."

The audience is mesmerized; some members seem pleased. Until McKeon got up to speak, Stokes's conviction appeared certain, but now the outcome is again in doubt. The trial has grown more fascinating than ever.

McKeon promises to prove that Fisk was armed, and he ascribes the silence of the defense till now on this point to reasonable prudence. "We were afraid to develop our case because we knew that perjury could be easily procured. It was for the purpose of preventing anyone from manufacturing testimony on the subject that we kept our own counsel."

McKeon artfully allows the jury a fallback position in case it doesn't accept the argument of Fisk's pistol packing. "Stokes might have been wrong, but he believed that his life was in danger. He had the hallucination that Fisk was about to jump upon him suddenly. He slept with his pistol under his pillow. Whether his belief was well founded or not makes no difference. I am sure he believed it, and if you are satisfied that he so believed, you are bound to acquit him. If you have reason to apprehend, from the desperate character of the man opposed to him, that he actually saw, or believed he saw, that man draw upon him, you will find him guiltless."

McKeon appeals to the jurors' humanity and to the spirit of the law. "Bear with us while we unfold this story to you. We ask you to believe us, and hear us in that spirit of mercy which the common law nobly, eloquently says would rather err on the side of mercy than on the side of justice."

25

McKeon's opening for Stokes puts New York in a frenzy of anticipation at what further twists the trial might take. When the newspapers report that the defense has listed Ned Stokes and Josie Mansfield as its principal witnesses, the prospect of seeing the two surviving parties to the infamous love triangle on the stand ratchets emotions still higher. Hours before the doors of the courtroom open the next day, the spectators line up. The police struggle to hold them back; most are turned away, only to linger outside the courthouse simply to be near the scene.

Josie's entry produces the most visible stir of the trial so far. She has remained in seclusion since the shooting, and today she wears a veil. But as the woman at the center of the case, she is the person everyone wants to see. Her veil imparts not mourning but mystery. She walks slowly to her place, aware of the attention she draws. She seems, beneath the veil, to relish it.

Stokes, by contrast, obviously wishes he were somewhere else. He is tense, and when he takes the stand as the first witness for the defense, he can hardly speak. He fidgets in his chair and repeatedly asks for water.

Defense counsel Lyman Tremain tries to calm him with easy questions. "You are the prisoner in this case?"

"Yes, sir."

"What is your age?"

"Thirty-one years."

"Where were you born?"

"In Philadelphia."

"How long did you reside there?"

"Twenty years."

"Where did you go from there?"

"I came to this city from the Philadelphia College, and went to live with my uncle, Peyton Gilbert, in Tenth Avenue."

"How long did you live with him?"

"I think two years."

"What business were you engaged in?"

"I went into the produce business, and continued in it till 1865. I then went into the oil refinery business over at Hunter's Point."

"How long did you continue there?"

"Up to the time Mr. Fisk turned me out of it."

The district attorney objects, and Judge Ingraham tells the jury to disregard the last statement.

Tremain asks the question again.

Stokes rephrases: "I continued in it up to 1870."

"When did you first become acquainted with Fisk?"

"I think in the month of July 1869."

"Where?"

"At the Erie Railroad office."

"Did you have any business relations with him prior to this alleged homicide?"

Objection; overruled.

"Yes, sir."

"State generally the character of those relations."

Objection; sustained.

Tremain recasts the question: "I mean the general business nature, without detail."

Objection; sustained.

"Had your relations been friendly and intimate?"

Objection; sustained.

Tremain appeals to Judge Ingraham. "Would it not be proper, Your Honor, to show the nature of the transactions with Fisk?"

"I don't think you have any right to go back two years," the judge replies.

Defense counsel McKeon interjects: "Can't we go on to show that for several years he has been endeavoring to get his legal rights, and in consequence of the corrupt judiciary he could not do it?"

Judge Ingraham evinces no response to this slap at the court system of which he is a part. Neither do the spectators, for conventional wisdom, bolstered by repeated experience, is that justice is for sale in New York and goes, as a matter of course, to the highest bidder. Ingraham merely inquires: "What has that to do with this transaction?"

"The operation of his mind," McKeon says. "We had got to a state of anarchy."

McKeon hasn't explicitly introduced insanity as a defense, in part because such defenses are comparatively novel in American jurisprudence and remain highly controversial. But his colleague Tremain essentially does so for him. "In all cases where a defense of insanity has been interposed," Tremain says, addressing Judge Ingraham, "the prisoner has been allowed to show the transactions between himself and the deceased in connection with other evidence to prove what effect they would be likely to produce." He cites the case of a woman who murdered her fiancé; her defense counsel showed the wrongs he had done her. "When we wanted to show that the prisoner was under apprehension of his life, and gave notice to his friends that if he should be found killed at any time, he wanted the burden of his death thrown upon the deceased, we were met by the assertion that we hadn't laid the foundation for it. Now we want to show that the doings of the deceased were such as to operate upon an excitable temperament, and how can we show their effect upon the mind of the prisoner, without proving all the circumstances that bore upon their relations? We want to show the power of Mr. Fisk with his Erie Railroad, with the judiciary, and that in consequence the prisoner had been repeatedly foiled in his attempts to procure justice."

Tremain looks to Judge Ingraham and then to the jury, before continuing. "If we show that the deceased had applied to the courts to obtain an injunction to take away the property of the prisoner—if this was followed up by suit after suit against him, tying him up in every shape and form, and that the deceased resorted to all means, legal and illegal, for the purpose of depriving him of his rights, and then we are able to follow it up by that proof of threats, pursuit by armed men of hostile intentions on the part of the deceased, all of which were known to the prisoner from his associations with the deceased, and through his friends, has not Your Honor to decide what proof we shall offer? Are we to be stopped here? Are we to be arrested and controlled in the order of our proofs, and prevented from laying that foundation which shall enable us to establish the theory of insanity? I submit that proof of their business relations ought to be received as bearing on the evidence of insanity. I think, also, we should be allowed to show that this prisoner knew the fact that Mr. Fisk was filled with hostility toward him, and that he entertained the most vindictive feelings against him."

William Beach, for the prosecution, doesn't like this loose definition of insanity. He objects that the defense is wandering far afield from Stokes's mental state at the moment of the crime. "Is there any possible pretense upon which it can be asserted that this prisoner at the time of this fatal act was laboring under any insanity or delusion? Is there any proof from the last witness, who was the last man who had an interview with him previous to the fatal act, that he was suffering from a disturbed mind—that there was any hallucination? On the contrary, he goes to this act perfectly cool, and when it is done he leaves it in the same unconcerned frame of mind. In answer to the remarks in regard to the corrupt judiciary, allow me to say that my friend is altogether mistaken in his idea of the course of this prisoner. It is enough to say that neither of the litigations between Fisk and Stokes was before either of the judges charged with malconduct. This idea of a corrupt judiciary having interfered to promote the purposes of Fisk in his litigations with this prisoner is entirely incorrect."

Tremain wants the judge to rein Beach in, but Ingraham lets Beach proceed. "It seems to me," the prosecution counsel asserts, "that these aspersions, not only upon the judiciary of the city, but also these unfounded and atrocious calumnies uttered against the dead Mr. Fisk are intended for an ulterior object—to affect the mind of this jury and to interfere with the course of justice. I knew the faults and the foibles of the man who is in his grave, and I know, also, that he was a man of large heart, and there are men who treasure him today in spite of the assaults of this defense, and I have no shame in uttering this justification of him here when he cannot answer for himself. I do not deny that under proper conditions it is competent for the defense to prove that the deceased was of a violent, dangerous, and malignant disposition, and on certain conditions this evidence is admissible; but the settled doctrine of the Court of Appeals is that the evidence cannot be admitted until a foundation has been laid; there must be circumstances that raise the question in regard to the danger of the murderer; he must show there was danger of these threats being carried into effect, and there was reasonable ground to believe that he stood in imminent peril of his life or limb."

Beach reads to the court from the opinion in *People* v. *Lamb,* a landmark homicide case, and glosses the finding: "In this case there was no pretense that the deceased was in a contentious mood. Why, sir, it would be one of the most atrocious propositions in the administration of criminal justice if a man who kills can justify himself by proving that he distrusted the temper or purpose of the man he slew. Did this prisoner mean to kill? That is the premeditation which the law requires. These rules are fixed, immutable, and I do not understand what these impassioned appeals from the leading counsel for the defense and these gross and atrocious narratives mean, unless it is to gather about this case a mist which shall interrupt the course of justice. There are responsibilities which rest with heavy weight upon the prosecution here; there is public justice to be conserved; there is the safety of a thousand lives to be protected. For if, under the circumstances of this case, this prisoner be justified in his act, there are a thousand ruffians in this community who will hasten to take vengeance in their own hands and make bloodier still the streets of your city, which is already running with blood."

Beach and Tremain appear willing to argue this point all day, but Judge Ingraham finally cuts them short. He tells the defense to move on.

Tremain resumes his questioning of Stokes, who seems somewhat calmer for the distraction. "Had your relations with Fisk been intimate, friendly?"

The prosecution objects; the question is excluded.

Tremain turns to Ingraham: "Do I understand we may now show the relations between the parties some time immediately preceding the occurrence?"

"At the *time* of the occurrence," Ingraham instructs.

Tremain turns back to Stokes. "What were Fisk's relations to you at the time of the alleged homicide?"

The prosecution objects. "The question is so general, so broad."

Tremain rephrases: "Were your relations with Fisk friendly or hostile at the time of the occurrence?"

"Very hostile."

"How long had they been so hostile? For some weeks or months?"

Objection, but Stokes answers: "Yes, they had been hostile since January 8, 18–"

"Stop! Stop!" the district attorney shouts.

Stokes tries again: "On the morning of the day in question, I had been before Justice Bixby as a witness. I had not seen Fisk since the opening night of *The Black Crook* some two or three weeks before. I had heard that he was sick then, so that at the time I passed the Opera House I had no expectation of seeing him. I think we left the court about two o'clock. We came downtown in a carriage together—District Attorney Fellows, Mr. McKeon, and myself. The case was one in which Josephine Mansfield was complainant; she left the court about the time the rest did and in company with her cousin, Mrs. Williams, in another carriage. We drove down to Delmonico's, at the corner of Broadway and Chambers Street. I remained there till half past two. I took oysters and a glass of ale with Mr. Sprague. After I took lunch at Delmonico's I went over to the office of Mr. Rufus Andrews, right opposite." Andrews is Stokes's attorney. "He told me there was no chance of any indictment being found against me, and advised me to go to Providence. I was not satisfied, so I went over to Judge Bixby, and he told me by all means to go to Providence. He said the indictment had been dismissed several times. I then got into a coupé and drove up to the Hoffman House. I went up to my room for some papers for this court of appeals in Providence. I then went down into the office. I found the dispatch there"—announcing his indictment.

"I object!" the district attorney interrupts.

"Oh, we can't get along a step without your perpetual 'I object. I object'?" McKeon replies.

Stokes speaks through the interruption: "I found that I had left some of the papers at Miss Mansfield's. I got into the coupé and drove there. When I arrived there I found her house all closed, the windows all shut. I thought she might be sick. I thought then I would not disturb her, but go on downtown."

McKeon has been watching the private counsel silently conferring on the prosecution side. "Is it quite proper for the counsel to be sitting there, winking and blinking at each other?" he asks of Judge Ingraham.

Beach, without waiting for Ingraham, responds that he is simply doing what the defense has been doing. "If you wink and blink, we shall wink and blink. And as I sit with my back to the jury, they cannot see me wink and blink."

Judge Ingraham shakes his head and motions for Stokes to continue.

"I told the driver to take me down to the corner of the Grand Central Hotel," Stokes says. Near the hotel he encountered a friend, a man named Bailey. "He asked me where I was going. I said to get some seats for *The Black Crook*. I asked him to go with me. He consented to do so. We walked across Amity Street. When we were about opposite the main entrance of the Grand Central, I noticed a lady standing in the window of this parlor"—he points to a diagram of the hotel's floor plan that has been placed before the court. "She was looking out of the window. I thought it was a lady I had met at Saratoga; I thought she recognized me. I asked Bailey if he would come over to the hotel. He refused to go. At that time we were talking about some business of my brother Horace. I walked part of the way back with him, I think half a block. I then crossed over to the ladies' entrance. The street was crowded with carriages; I might have run a little in crossing.

"I walked into the ladies' entrance and up the stairs. A boy was standing on the ladder, cleaning the windows on the stairs. When I looked into the parlor at the lady, I found I was not acquainted with her. She did not recognize me. I walked along the main hall"—he points to the diagram of the hotel. "I walked along this corridor as far as I could go. It was the first time I had ever been on the second floor of the Grand Central Hotel. I looked into this parlor, then I walked back again. A lady passed me coming out of the dining room and went upstairs.

"I was going down these stairs again; I had got down three or four stairs when I saw Fisk coming up; he sprang up to this platform; he pulled out a pistol from behind; I was then on the same line with him. I said, 'Don't fire.' I jumped across to the left hand; I placed my hand on the banisters; I pulled my pistol and fired."

"You were intending to pass him?"

"Yes, I was going right out of the entrance. This boy Redmond was not inside at all; he was outside. I had no idea at first it was Mr. Fisk; I did not know it till I got four or five steps down."

"Why did you fire?"

"Because I knew he wanted to kill me. He had his pistol out; he had it in his hand."

"You are convinced he had a pistol?"

"He had a silver-plated pistol."

"Did you believe he was going to fire at you?"

"He had the pistol cocked; then I fired. I could not

have had time to pull out my pistol if it had not been in my overcoat. He staggered a little. He had his pistol in both hands. After that he cried out, 'I am shot.' I turned back. I walked up the stairs. There was nobody there. The boy Redmond was in the street. I dropped my pistol between the head of the stairs and Room No. 219. It fell out of my hand. I met Mr. Hill. He said, 'What's up?' I said, 'There is a man shot.' When I got to the foot of the stairs I said, 'Will you go for a doctor? There is a man shot.' Then I heard somebody say, 'Here, they want you.' I turned round and went with him. Two or three then came up. After that, what took place I really don't know. I know when I was taken and confronted with Fisk."

Stokes pauses to catch his breath. The courtroom is absolutely still. Whether the jury and spectators believe Stokes is impossible to say, but they are riveted by his story.

Tremain asks the witness to elaborate on this second meeting with Fisk.

"The officer took me into the room with Fisk," Stokes says. "He was sitting in the center of the sofa. He had his coat off and was in his shirtsleeves. He said, 'That is Mr. Stokes,' and dropped his eyes. He was looking very bad. I was going to ask him to exonerate me."

"Stop! Stop!" the prosecution objects. "We have nothing to do with your intentions. What occurred?"

Tremain prompts Stokes: "Did you understand him then as charging you with shooting?"

"No. He said, 'That is Mr. Stokes.' "

"Now before you went into that house, had you any knowledge, information, or suspicion that Fisk was there?"

"Not the slightest. I did not see any carriage of Fisk's there. I supposed that he was sick. I had no knowledge that he was going to that hotel that afternoon in his carriage."

"When you went toward the private ladies' entrance to go out, had you any expectation of meeting Fisk?"

"No."

"When you came down those steps, had you any knowledge that Fisk was in the house?"

"No."

"Did you go searching about in the hall and parlors, crouching and bending about?"

"No."

"Did you say before firing, 'Now, I have got you'?"

"I made no such remark."

"You cried out to Fisk not to fire?"

"That is the only word I spoke. I was searched downstairs for a pistol, the pistol I bought on Broadway, next to Delmonico's."

"For what purpose?"

"I object!" the district attorney shouts.

Tremain looks at him and at Judge Ingraham. "What for?" he says. "We offer to show that by reason of threats that had been communicated to him he got that pistol."

Ingraham sustains the objection.

Tremain resumes the questioning. "Did you have a cane in your hand?"

"Yes, a light walking stick. I had on a large pair of dogskin driving gloves."

"When you fired?"

"Yes, and I also had on a very large driving coat of Irish frieze. I had it made to drive out over the roads with in rough weather. It was very large and clumsy. It was seven or eight inches larger than an ordinary walking coat."

"Before you met Mr. Fisk at the hotel, had any warning or information been communicated to you of threats made by Mr. Fisk to do you injury?"

"I object!" the prosecutor cries.

The judge asks Tremain: "Within what time?"

"Within a month; for a long time before."

Ingraham overrules the objection.

Tremain asks Stokes: "Had you been warned or informed of threats to take your life before this meeting?"

"I had."

"What was the nature of the threats communicated?"

Objection! Overruled.

"Had you heard that Fisk had made threats against your life?"

"Numerous times."

"When was the last warning that you received of his threatening to kill you prior to the homicide?"

Stokes reflects for a moment. "I think it was December 20."

"Was this the first time you had seen him after you heard of that threat?"

"I think it was."

"What knowledge did you possess at the time of this meeting in relation to the character of the deceased?"

Objection! Overruled.

"Did you know what the character of the deceased was?"

"Yes, sir."

"What was it?"

Prosecution counsel Beach interrupts. "Define as to what," he demands.

Tremain looks to the judge: "Do you want me to lead the witness?"

"Yes, so far," Ingraham replies.

Tremain turns to Stokes. "As to disposition and temperament," he says.

"I knew him to be a very vindictive, unscrupulous, desperate character, a man who stopped at nothing to carry out his designs at all hazards."

"Before you met the deceased on this occasion, speak whether recently, and when, you had been followed by ruffianly looking persons whom you believed to be sent by the deceased to pursue you."

Objection; sustained.

"Whom you were informed were sent by Fisk to pursue you?"

Objection; excluded. Rephrased. Excluded. Rephrased again: "Had you, nights and days for a long time prior to this meeting, traveled in covered carriages from fears and apprehensions that you would be attacked at the instigation of Fisk?"

"I did. I always traveled in carriages, night and day ever since my trouble with Fisk, and for that reason."

"For how long?"

"I should think for twelve months, if not longer."

"Did you get persons to go with you and protect you?"

"Yes, sir."

"Had Mr. Fisk told you prior to the meeting that he had a plan all laid for railroading you to state prison?"

"Yes, sir, he told me he had it all arranged with the district attorney's to railroad me to state prison, and I communicated it last summer to Assistant District Attorney Fellows, at Saratoga."

"Never mind that."

"Mr. Fellows said it wasn't so."

Tremain turns to the court stenographer: "Don't take that. It is not responsive to the question." He asks Stokes: "Did he say to you at any time that they had graveyards for those who crossed their track?"

"Yes, sir."

"Was it at a dinner party?"

"Yes, sir."

"Where?"

"At Miss Mansfield's."

The audience sits up at Josie's name, and they look toward her veiled figure. She evinces no reaction.

"Who were present?"

"Mrs. Williams, and I think another gentleman."

"Who was that?"

Stokes lowers his voice: "Judge Barnard."

A loud murmur in the court at the statement that the judge was consorting with the seductress, or at least was enjoying her company.

"Never mind that," Tremain orders the court stenographer. He asks Stokes: "How long had you labored under these apprehensions of attacks you have spoken of–how long before the meeting?"

"Since the arrest. He had me arrested once and put in jail. Ever since that day–I think it was January 1871."

Tremain asks whether Fisk had ever said to Stokes: "We rule New York with a rod of iron, as completely as Robespierre ruled France."

Objection; excluded.

Had Fisk told Stokes that one man who had been prepared to testify against him had been put on a ship bound for China?

Objection; excluded.

Had Fisk and his ruffians forcibly seized Stokes's oil refinery in January 1871?

Objection; excluded.

Tremain says he has no further questions and sits down.

Stokes takes a breath and asks for more water.

26

The prosecution cannot let Stokes's version of the shooting go unchallenged, of course. Assistant District Attorney Garvin commences the cross-examination. "When did you purchase the pistol you had on this occasion?" he asks Stokes.

"I think about six months before the occurrence."

"Do you recollect whether you bought more than one?"

"Only one. I bought another at this place previously."

"Did you ever carry a pistol before one or the other of these two pistols?"

"No, I never carried a pistol until I became afraid of Fisk."

"What kind of overcoat had you?"

"A light overcoat."

"The one you generally wore?"

"I seldom wore it. It was a conspicuous overcoat. I got

it more especially as I intended to go to Europe, and I thought it a good overcoat to go there with."

"What kind of hat did you wear?"

"A black high hat."

"Do you know who the lady was you went to see?"

"No, sir. I should think she was a guest of the hotel."

"Did you ever ascertain what was her name?"

"No, sir."

"Do you remember when you came to the head of the stairs seeing anybody there or in the hall leading to the dining room?"

"I remember a good many persons in the hall leading to the dining room."

"You say that Redmond was on the stairs when the first shot was fired?"

"No, I thought Redmond was between the first and second door. I have an idea he saw me, because he described my having hands on the banisters. I recollected somebody going downstairs and out, and I had an idea it was him."

"Had you ever been up those stairs before?"

"I had never been on the second floor of the Grand Central Hotel in my life."

"Was any word spoken by Fisk?"

"No, sir."

"By you?"

"All I said to him was 'Don't fire.' "

"You have a pretty clear recollection of everything that occurred until you got downstairs?"

"Yes, sir, although I was somewhat bewildered."

"How far up the stairs had Fisk got when the firing took place?"

"He was on the first platform. As soon as he got on the platform he pulled his pistol out."

"Did he fire?"

"I would not like to swear whether he fired his pistol or not. If he did, it was not pointed at me. I did not see him extend his arm at all."

"You intended to shoot at that time?"

"Yes, sir."

"And did shoot?"

"Yes, sir."

"Did you know your pistol was loaded?"

"Yes, sir."

"How lately had you loaded it?"

"Not since the time I bought it, six months before."

"At the time you fired, you intended to hit Mr. Fisk?"

"Yes, sir."

The district attorney, seeming happy that he has cast doubt on Stokes's story—Did Stokes see a gun in Fisk's hand or not? Was Redmond on the street or on the stairs? Was there really a woman who caused Stokes to enter the Grand Central?—lets the prisoner step down.

27

The defense next calls Josie Mansfield. Spectators, jurymen, lawyers, the judge all watch the veiled woman as she rises from her seat and walks slowly to the witness box. "Mrs. Mansfield's dress was rather *décolleté*," a *World* reporter torn between titillation and scandalization will recount in the next day's paper. "Her thin muslin over-shirt set off her plump shoulders. The region that laryn-gitis attacks was only covered by a heavy gold chain and an amulet or cross. She had heavy earrings of a blue color. A high black hat, surmounted by a blue feather, gave her what printers might call a 'bold-face-extended' look. A heavy wisp of hair hung free from among her braids. A black lace shawl was cast loosely over her shoulders. On her arms were heavy gold bracelets, and on her hands violet-colored gloves." Josie lifts her veil to acknowledge the judge and the jury; all in the courtroom lean forward to see the face of the woman at the heart of the drama that has sent one man to the grave and has put another on a path that might end at the gallows.

"On the 6th of last January," defense counsel John Townsend asks, "were you engaged in any proceedings in the Yorkville Police Court?"

"Yes, sir, a libel suit against Mr. Fisk," Josie responds in a soft voice. "The proceedings were commenced some time in November, I believe. I was in court on the 6th of January. Colonel Fisk was not there. Mr. Stokes was there. On that day I was very ill. I left the court about two o'clock, in company with my cousin."

"When had you prior to that time seen Mr. Fisk?"

"About three weeks before."

"Where?"

"At my own house."

"Was the interview brought about through his agency?"

"He wrote me a note asking for an interview."

Townsend hands her a note; Josie identifies it as the one in question. Townsend starts to read the note but the prosecution objects and Judge Ingraham sustains.

"When did you receive that note?"

"About the 15th of December. Colonel Fisk called on me about half past ten o'clock that night."

"Did he at that interview make any threats against Stokes?"

"He said that unless I returned to him he should kill Mr. Stokes."

The spectators whisper excitedly; Judge Ingraham glowers at them.

"Did he at that time exhibit any pistol?" Townsend asks.

"He did. It was a handsome pistol, silver mounted, with a pearl handle. I took it in my hand and examined it."

"Did you communicate what Mr. Fisk said, to the prisoner, Stokes?"

"I did. A day or two afterward I told Mr. Stokes that Mr. Fisk had called upon me to see if I would not release him from that case in the Police Court, and promised to give me all the money I was suing him for, but I told him I would not release him unless he would publicly acknowledge that King's affidavit was a fraud and a libel. He said that as far as he personally was concerned he did not care so much, but there were so many people involved that he could not make such a statement. I refused to withdraw the suit unless he would acknowledge that I was in the right. He said then that I must bear the consequences. I said, 'What?' He drew his revolver and said, 'I shall shoot Stokes.' I said, 'Oh, no, you won't do anything like that.' He said, 'Well, you will see. There will be blood shed before you get through. You better release me. I beg of you not to appear against me again.' I said, 'I most assuredly shall, because I shall be vindicated in this affair.' Mr. Fisk remained about half an hour. No one else was present. When he spoke of shooting Stokes, he spoke in a very decided manner, as if he meant to do what he said."

"Did you give Mr. Stokes any advice at the time you made this statement to him?"

"I told him he should be more careful than he had been. I knew what a dangerous man Fisk was. He had, prior to that time, made use of threats nearly every time he came to my house after we separated."

"State what you said in regard to what Colonel Fisk said in reference to the disposal of Eaton."

The reference to the assault on Dorman Eaton stirs the crowd as it had done during the opening remarks of the defense. It also moves the prosecution to object. Judge Ingraham overrules.

Townsend rephrases: "Did you ever state to Stokes at any time what Colonel Fisk had said in reference to his being disposed of in the same way that Eaton had been?"

"Yes, sir."

"What did you tell him?"

"I had already told him what had been done to Eaton, and I told him how easily it could be done to him."

Judge Ingraham asks for clarification: "Fisk told you, and you told that to Stokes?"

"Yes, sir."

"What else did you say to Mr. Stokes?"

"That Mr. Fisk said that he and Gould and another party had arranged to attack Mr. Eaton. I told Mr. Stokes that he should be very careful of himself, that Mr. Eaton would be disposed of next day. I told him this because he doubted Mr. Fisk's power."

Townsend resumes the defense's questioning: "When you saw a pistol in Fisk's possession about the 15th of December, had you seen one prior to that time in his possession?"

"Yes, sir."

"On how many occasions?"

"Several."

"Was any person present at any time when Fisk showed these besides yourself?"

"Yes, sir."

"Who?"

"My cousin, Mrs. Williams."

The defense concludes its questioning of Josie, and Townsend takes his seat. District Attorney Garvin rises and approaches the witness to conduct the cross-examination. "You say you saw him have a pistol on several different occasions?" he asks her, regarding Fisk. "Was it always the same pistol?"

"I think so."

"How long do you speak of?"

"Ever since we came from Jersey City in 1868."

"How many pistols did you see him have?"

"I should suppose eight or ten."

"Do you know of his carrying pistols, or did he always leave them at home?"

"He carried them, but not always. He carried them on several occasions—on Black Friday, for instance, he carried a pistol for a long time. And when we went up to Albany on the Susquehanna business."

"Do you know whether he carried a pistol on other occasions?"

"Yes, sir, when we were in Jersey City, and when we went away traveling—about the month I left him."

"What month was that?"

"September 1870."

"How long did you say you had been acquainted with Stokes?"

"Since February 1869."

"And with Fisk?"

"Since February 1867."

"How long had you resided in that house?"

"Three years the first day of that month."

"Was that the house where you say you had the conversation with Colonel Fisk?"

"Yes, sir."

"On this day of the examination"—before Judge Bixby in the Yorkville court—"did you leave anybody at your house except the servants?"

"No, sir, the house was closed that day, and when I came home I had a terrible headache—terrible headache. No one called that afternoon except beggars, no visitors that afternoon at all."

"When did you first hear of the shooting?"

"Not until between five and six o'clock."

"How did you hear of it?"

"A newspaper reporter came to the house for intelligence, and my cousin went to the door. She came and told me of it. I did not believe it then."

"Have you ever seen the prisoner since that day?"

"Never until today."

"Did you see Fisk after the shooting, and before his death?"

"No, sir."

"Did you see him after his death?"

"No, sir."

The district attorney indicates that he has no more questions, and Josie steps down.

28

The testimony of Stokes and Josie has contradicted the prosecution's assertion of cold-blooded murder. Stokes feared for his life before entering the Grand Central Hotel on the day of the shooting; in the stairwell he saw Fisk pull a pistol, or thought he did; his shots were fired in self-defense. So Stokes has said. Josie has corroborated Stokes's reason for fear and Fisk's possession of a gun.

But, doubtless worried that the jury will judge the siren and her paramour less than credible, the defense hedges its bets. It summons expert witnesses who suggest that Fisk died not of shock from the gunshot wounds but from the opium administered for the pain. "A man in the prime of life, in unusually sound health, receives a severe injury from a pistol-shot wound," defense counsel Townsend says to Dr. John M. Carnochan, physician and surgeon. "That man being a man of temperate habits in the use of spirituous liquors, the shock is recovered from, his pulse seventy-six, respiration twenty-four, the wound having been inflicted about half past four in the afternoon, his pulse having fallen very low, about half past six his pulse is seventy-six and respiration twenty-four, and about half past ten his pulse is natural and respiration normal, his intelligence good—would you apprehend any danger from shock?"

"When we see a patient recovering from shock, his functions again working naturally," Carnochan replies, "we would infer that there is no immediate apprehension of collapse."

Townsend asks Dr. Benjamin Macready the same questions and receives a similar negative. "What *was* the cause of the death of Mr. Fisk?" Townsend then inquires.

"I have no doubt that the cause of death was directly the influence of opium," Macready answers. "It was not shock. It was opium and nothing else."

The defense returns to its argument that Stokes was insane, at least temporarily, at the time of the shooting. To establish a pattern of unbalance, his lawyers summon Edward H. Stokes, the seventy-two-year-old father of the prisoner. "Mr. Stokes, state to your recollection whether or not you have discovered any change in the conduct of the prisoner, and if so where and of what character?"

"From the time of his first trouble with Mr. Fisk, six or eight months before his arrest."

"Will you state to the jury what those appearances or evidences were?"

"He complained of a great pain in his head." The elder Stokes covers his eyes and cradles his head as if in severe pain. "There was an entire unfixedness of purpose; he would propose a thing one moment, and the next he would fly off on another subject. On one or two occasions, when I would proffer any advice, he would seem very much excited and very disrespectful, different from his former behavior."

"Did you notice anything peculiar in his countenance or his eye?"

"Yes, sir."

"What was it?"

"I can hardly describe it, rather different from what I had ever seen before."

"Have there been cases of insanity in your family?"

Mr. Stokes winces visibly. "Yes, sir. I had a brother who died in the insane asylum."

"Any other cases?"

"I had a sister who became imbecile."

Nancy Stokes, the mother of the prisoner, testifies that her son had grown very agitated after his tangle with Fisk. "His eyes had a wild appearance that I had never seen before," she says.

Howard Stokes, the prisoner's brother, describes a particular manifestation of Stokes's nervousness. "He told me he couldn't pass a night without the pistol, and hadn't for some time."

Ned Stokes squirms under the testimony of those who

know him best. The unconcern he affected just after Fisk's death has vanished; escaping from this trial with his life seems to demand surrendering his self-respect. The bargain might be necessary, but he doesn't like it.

29

Tremain ties together the defense's lines of reasoning in his concluding argument. "On the poor, feeble words that may fall from my lips," he tells the jury, "rest not only the fate of this young man with a future opening bright and beautiful before him, but little past the age of thirty, but also whether the blow shall be struck by your hands that will place upon that innocent child of his the stigma of being denounced as the son of a murderer; and whether his wife shall be hereafter pointed out as the widow of a murderer; and finally whether the gray hairs of this old father and mother shall be brought down in sorrow to the grave.

"There is a great disparity of forces here in this struggle. The prisoner, single-handed and alone, is struggling for his life against the full power of this gigantic commonwealth. Arrayed against him stands the public prosecutor. At his beck the whole police force of the city is ready to summon witnesses. The treasury of the state, the whole taxable power, the whole taxable property, is subject to the will of the public prosecutor. He comes here clothed with tenfold more power and influence before a jury than I can possibly collect, and then, in addition to all that, he has been aided by the learning, the ability, and the wisdom of two of the ablest members of our profession. The contest is an unequal one, and unless the prisoner's defense is one that is sustained by the power of truth, he can scarcely expect that, in such a mighty contest, he will not be driven to the wall. But if he has the truth on his side, then I care not what powers are brought against him."

Tremain sets out a series of propositions: "That the jury should not find the prisoner guilty of murder unless they are satisfied that he killed the deceased with premeditated design to effect his death; that the deceased died from the effects of a pistol-shot wound; that there was no justifiable cause of firing the pistol; and at the time the prisoner was not insane." If the jury entertains a reasonable doubt on any of these points, it must find Ned Stokes not guilty.

Tremain reiterates the arguments against each of these points. Stokes did not go to the Grand Central Hotel seeking Fisk; on the contrary, the meeting there was accidental. Fisk's death was the result of an overdose of opium, not of the gunshot wounds. Stokes had ample reason to believe that Fisk intended to harm him, culminating in Stokes's perception—whether accurate or not—that Fisk had drawn a pistol and was about to fire. Fisk's persecutions of Stokes had driven Stokes out of his right mind.

Tremain recapitulates the testimony of Josie Mansfield about Fisk's repeated threats against Stokes, and he asserts that the prosecution has utterly failed to rebut this testimony. So have Fisk's friends failed to defend their deceased partner, by their conspicuous absence at the trial and from the prosecution's list of witnesses. "Where is Jay Gould? Where is William M. Tweed? Where are those men that knew him in life and had enjoyed his hospitalities or his bounty? Where are the men who ate those splendid state dinners that he loved to give? Was there not one to be found who would say a word for their fallen chief?"

Some in the courtroom nod and exchange looks at the mention of Gould and Tweed, as if to second the query about their absence. Others stay focused on Tremain.

Tremain takes care not to assert that Fisk deserved killing, but he says that a violent death for such a man should come as no surprise. "The power of this man, through the Erie corporation, with its arms extending all over this country, with its thousands of employees and hundreds of millions of capital, and its many branches wielded by him and his associates—Rome, in the days of her decline, with all the examples of profligacy and licentiousness on the part of her nobility, never presented such instances as is shown in the life and career of this man. Do you ask me again whether I justify murder without any sense of imminent and impending danger? No. But God moves by laws. Men who live in violation of His laws, sooner or later, although they may flourish and prosper, will fail. It is well that it is so, for the successful career of a man who tramples under foot all laws human and divine would set at naught the teachings of the Bible and the instruction of father and mother around the domestic fireside. He who takes the sword shall fall by the sword. Men who live a life of violence are ever liable to fall victims to violence."

Tremain asks the jury to do its duty, no more and no less. And part of its duty is to inform justice with humility. This is a fundamental premise of the law. "It is found in the very unanimity which requires the agreeing of all the twelve jurors before convicting. It is found in the doctrine that it is better that ninety-nine guilty men should go free than that one innocent should suffer. It is found in the rule that if there is reasonable doubt on the whole case, it is your duty to acquit. And finally, more clearly perhaps than in any other case, it is found in the great principle that he is to be tried by twelve men with human hearts and human sympathies, with that natural reluctance which exists against consigning a man to the gallows."

30

Tremain's speech moves the spectators. Several exhibit agreement; many scrutinize Stokes less skeptically than before. The whispers sound softer, as if the whisperers are more willing to allow for human weakness.

District Attorney Garvin acknowledges the shift as he begins the conclusion for the state. "All the sympathy of the jury, the audience, the court, prosecuting officers, and counsel is with the living man, with the relatives that surround him and the associations with which he is connected," Garvin says. This is only natural. So is the tendency to devalue those who cannot appear in court. "The dead are forgotten; their good deeds are buried with them, and their bad deeds, if they have any, are brought to the surface in the course of a trial like this. Every stain on their character is referred to. Every single thing that can be brought to light against them is displayed in characters of living fire."

Yet the quality of the life of the deceased is not the issue here, Garvin continues, but the manner of its termination. "He was struck down while going up the stairway into the ladies' entrance of the Grand Central Hotel, and sent into eternity by a pistol shot by the prisoner, who pleads for mercy, who asks for reasonable doubt in his favor, who asks for sympathy at the hands of this jury, and who prays through counsel for the right to be heard. All these for him. Poor Fisk has no jury, no counsel, no friends. Among strangers, no human being that he ever saw before, so far as we know, except the employees of this hotel, except the prisoner, who at the head of the stairs took his life in a moment. This is not disputed. This is admitted, and nobody denies. He swears to it himself. Yet he stands here asking for protection."

The defense has made its case on three allegedly mitigating grounds, Garvin says. "First, insanity—want of responsibility—whatever it may be called. Second, that Fisk did not die of the wound that was inflicted upon him by this pistol shot. And third, self-defense."

The district attorney serially dissects the defense arguments. Regarding insanity: "Is there any doubt that this man started on this day, came down from Delmonico's to Andrews's office, to Bixby's court, and the Hoffman House and the Erie Railway office, and the corner of Fourth Street, to Chamberlain & Dodge's, and to the Grand Central Hotel, and performed this deed? Anybody say he is guilty of any symptoms of insanity? Anything said or done by him that afternoon, or that day, or that week, that should indicate that he is not a sane man and knew what he is doing? Every step that he took that day, every word he said, and everything that he did, only goes to confirm the idea that he was just as responsible as he is today."

As to the cause of death, Garvin reminds the jurors that while the doctors for the defense have asserted that shock from the gunshot wound was not the cause of death, other equally distinguished physicians have asserted that the shock *was* the cause of death. The jurors must make up their own minds—and recall that without the gunshot, fired by Stokes, the issue of the technical cause of death never would have arisen.

In the matter of self-defense, Stokes claims to have seen a pistol in Fisk's hand. "Where is the pistol Fisk is alleged to have had? Was it dropped anywhere, and why was it not found? If the shot was fired in self-defense, why did Stokes not say so to the crowds on the spot? Why did he not say so to Hart when he charged him with shooting Fisk? Why did he not say so to the deceased when brought before him for recognition?"

And what is the evidence for the existence of a pistol in Fisk's hand? "The only testimony to that effect was by the prisoner, confirmed by a woman connected with these two men, one of whom she had brought to death, the other to this peril." He asks the jury to disregard Josie Mansfield's testimony as entirely self-interested and wholly unreliable. He quotes Proverbs: "Deliver me from the strange woman. Her house inclineth unto death, and her paths to the dead."

The arguments of the defense have failed, Garvin concludes. The responsibility of the jury is to judge not the dead man or his associates but the prisoner. "I care nothing for the Erie ring or the Tammany ring or any other ring. I care for right, justice, and truth." If the jurors have doubts regarding the testimony of particular witnesses, let them ignore it. "There is evidence enough beside." The question is simple: "If there was a killing without provocation it was murder."

Garvin reminds the jurors that they bear great responsibility. New York is a dangerous place; he notes a recent series of violent murders that have set the entire community on edge. "If you release this man, blood will continue to flow in our streets."

The accused has acted; now he must accept the consequence of his actions. "By the law he is to be judged; by the law he is to be punished."

31

Judge Ingraham has been an intermittent presence in the trial so far, letting the lawyers predominate. Now he takes command as he gives the jury its charge. "I know that you are acting here in the performance of a disagreeable task," he says. "But I know that you feel you have a duty to perform—a duty you owe to the public, a duty you owe to yourselves."

The jurors must be guided solely by the evidence adduced at the trial. "Banish from your minds sympathy for the prisoner, his family, or his friends. Banish from your minds any prejudice existing *against* the prisoner. Banish also from your minds anything which will tend to the favor or disfavor of the prisoner, other than what has been derived from the consideration of the case."

The jurors must keep the fundamental issue clearly in mind. "We have a simple question to try, and you have a simple answer to render on that question, and that is, whether this prisoner is guilty or innocent of the charge preferred against him." The charge is murder in the first degree. "Murder is the killing of a human being without excuse or justification, with the intent to take life." Much of the case as presented turns on the matter of intent. "You are to form an opinion as to the intent of this man from his acts, conduct, and declarations, by all the circumstances connected with the incidents for which he is on trial." The prosecution has alleged that Stokes went to the hotel intending to shoot Fisk. "If you come to the conclusion that he had that intent when he came there and carried it out, and you don't find any circumstance to warrant you seeing that he was justified or excused in that act, or that there is some other cause that rendered him irresponsible, then you will find him guilty."

Judge Ingraham explains the law touching the issue of the cause of death. If the gunshot wound was mortal—that is, if it would have caused death in any event—the matter of whether the death at the precise moment it came was caused by shock or by opium is immaterial. The judge notes that none of the physicians has asserted that Fisk could have recovered. In other words, they have agreed that the wound was indeed mortal.

The defense has argued that Stokes credibly feared for his life. Ingraham reminds the jurors that Stokes and Josie Mansfield have been the principal witnesses to this effect. The jury must decide whether to believe them.

On the insanity plea, he notes, the defendant is the sole material witness. Again the jury must decide.

As in every case, he concludes his charge, the defendant must receive the benefit of reasonable doubt.

≈ 32 ≈

Judge Ingraham finishes at half past two in the afternoon of July 13. The jurors file out and begin their deliberations. An hour passes, then another. At a few minutes before five, they return to the courtroom to ask the judge to define "premeditation." He does so and they retire once more. At seven Ingraham recalls them to the courtroom and asks whether they have reached a verdict. Their foreman says they have not. The judge orders them sequestered for the night. He sends Stokes back to the Tombs. The bailiff clears the courtroom.

The next day is Sunday, when New York's courts are supposed to rest. But there is no rest in this case. The Sunday papers are filled with the latest accounts from the courtroom, and the state legislature has approved a special statute allowing Judge Ingraham to declare Sunday's meeting of the court an extension of Saturday's session.

The spectators line up early to learn Stokes's fate. Perhaps because his recent testimony has reminded the city of his attractiveness to the opposite sex, perhaps because Josie's appearance has touched a feminine nerve, the crowd today is mostly women. Along with the men in the crowd, they have neglected church in favor of the criminal court. Women and men alike try to ignore the rising heat of the midsummer morning.

The ladies are admitted to the courtroom first; after they have entered, the few remaining seats are allowed to the men. Those persons denied admission mill around outside the court, growing hotter by the minute but assuming that the news of the verdict will be swiftly relayed from inside. Speculation is rampant regarding the jury's decision; fittingly, for a case involving Fisk, wagers are exchanged.

Ingraham enters the courtroom as the clock chimes eleven. Stokes is brought in after the judge sits down. The prisoner is pale and drawn; as he sinks into his seat a heavy breath escapes his lips.

The judge summons the jurors; the bailiff guides them to their box. The audience examines the jurors, trying to determine whether they have reached a verdict and what it might be. Stokes alone refuses to look toward the jury. He fixes his gaze on the table in front of him.

The judge asks the foreman if the jurors have reached a conclusion. The foreman says they have not.

Stokes looks up and toward the jury. The beginning of a smile flits across his face.

The foreman adds, "There is no probability that we can agree, not the least chance. We stand exactly where we stood last night."

Stokes's smile broadens.

Judge Ingraham shakes his head. "I hardly feel at liberty to discharge you yet. This case has lasted nearly three weeks, and it would not be proper to let you go without giving this case further consideration." He orders the jury to retire once more.

The spectators shift in their seats and mutter among themselves, but few leave. Those outside the court, where a slight motion of the summer air moderates the heat, begin to think they were lucky not to get in.

The clock on the courtroom wall ticks slowly. Noon comes and goes. The heat continues to mount. Few in the room want to leave and risk missing the most exciting verdict in New York in decades. But the afternoon heat, the spectators' growing fatigue, and eventually their hunger gradually diminish their ranks. Late in the day word spreads that Judge Ingraham has gone home to his house in Harlem. Calculating that under the best of circumstances news that the jury has come to a verdict will take an hour to reach him and he will require another hour to return, the remaining spectators conclude that he won't be back this evening, and they go home, too.

33

On Monday the curious return in greater numbers than ever. All seem certain that the trial will come to a conclusion this day, and probably this morning. The court officers apparently expect a quick verdict, for, in contrast to previous days, when they valiantly held the masses back, today they let everyone in. The seats are taken in an instant after the ten o'clock opening of the doors; the comparative laggards clog the aisles, crowd the entrances, and press close behind the tables where the defendant and the lawyers sit.

Stokes again seems hopeful, but his weariness is apparent. He chats casually with Tremain and McKeon but without any real spark. He seems exhausted and old; observers in the courtroom can hardly imagine that this is the same man who set Josie Mansfield's young heart racing.

Judge Ingraham enters at ten thirty. The bailiff summons the jurors. Their names are called; each signifies his presence. Ingraham asks the foreman if they have agreed on a verdict.

The foreman replies that they have not. Their positions remain unchanged from Saturday. They have argued and argued, but their differences are irreconcilable.

Ingraham nods gravely. He reiterates why he has held them so long, citing the seriousness of the offense and the importance of the trial. But he accepts the foreman's judgment that agreement is impossible. He thanks the jury members for their diligent service and dismisses them. The trial has failed.

Newsmen buttonhole the jurors as they leave the courtroom. No vow of secrecy binds them, and various members explain that on the first ballot, taken thirty minutes after they received their charge from Judge Ingraham, seven voted to convict on first-degree murder, while two insisted on the lesser crime of manslaughter—an alternative allowable under New York law. Three contended that the homicide was justified. The five dissenters joined forces around manslaughter, but there the deliberations stuck. Thirty-six hours later they remained stuck.

Stokes greets the verdict with tempered relief. He will not hang, not yet anyway. But neither will he be released. The deadlocked jury leaves him in the same position he has been in for six months—and in the same location: Judge Ingraham orders him back to the Tombs.

34

The city sighs unhappily at the result. No verdict is the worst verdict of all. Conviction has been preferred by those who disbelieve Stokes and Josie or, for one reason or another, admire Fisk. Acquittal suits those who find the Stokes-Mansfield version credible or who think Fisk had it coming. A mistrial yields no satisfaction whatever.

But court watchers in New York are not entirely bereft. Bill Tweed hasn't committed any capital crimes, so far as investigators of the Tammany ring can tell, yet he has committed innumerable offenses against property and propriety. For years Tweed and the ring have been constructing a new county courthouse for New York, and the longer they have built, the further the work appears from completion and the more money the project absorbs. The projected price tag of a quarter-million dollars has swollen past thirteen million, and the building remains unfinished. Invoices for the work have gradually come to light: $8,000 apiece for windows, $1.5 million for plumbing and lighting fixtures, $500,000 paid to one plasterer for some interior work and then $1 million to the same plasterer to redo the work, $800,000 to a carpenter, lesser sums to several dead men kept on the payroll. The contractors themselves haven't pocketed the greatest part of this money; most gets kicked back to Tweed and the ring, who have grown immensely wealthy off the public pork.

The grafting attracts attention. Thomas Nast draws pictures for *Harper's Weekly*; it was Nast who created the American version of Santa Claus, with rosy cheeks, fat belly, and full beard. And it is Nast who goes after Tweed. The Tammany boss actually does look like Santa Claus, but Nast draws him darker and much more dangerous. The *Times*, meanwhile, has gathered the story of the courthouse fraud, employing leaks from Tammany insiders who wanted a larger share of the graft. *Times* publisher George Jones knows a good story when he discovers one, and he releases the tale of the Tweed scandal in several parts, to maximize its effect on circulation.

Tweed and the ring respond by offering Jones a million dollars to kill the story. Jones rejects the offer—and adds it to the story. Tweed offers Thomas Nast half a million, which is likewise spurned. Tweed takes Nast's rejection harder. "I don't care a straw for your newspaper articles," he says. "My constituents don't know how to read, but they can't help seeing them damned pictures."

"Tweed and his gang are doomed," Governor Samuel Tilden, who has been elected on a catch-the-crooks platform, promises. "Before many days pass it will be made so hot for the arch robber that New York will not hold him." A grand jury, convened amid the Stokes proceedings, delivers a two-hundred-count indictment against Tweed and the ring. Readers of the New York papers catch the latest developments in the Stokes case one day and in the Tweed case the next. Most know that Tweed consorted with Fisk before the latter's demise; many guess that the death of the one has made the fall of the other more likely.

35

Stokes's second trial starts in December 1872. The lawyers are the same as before, but the judge is different. Douglas Boardman suffers neither fools nor feckless jurors; he is determined that there will be a verdict this time, and he holds the two sides to a swifter selection of a jury and a closer adherence to their central arguments. The testimony recapitulates what has gone before; little new evidence is adduced.

On January 5, 1873, the defense concludes its arguments. Lyman Tremain stresses the doctrine of reasonable doubt. The prosecution summarizes the state's case, with counsel William Beach asserting that any doubt of Stokes's guilt is *un*reasonable. Judge Boardman charges the jury. He reminds the members that Stokes, not Fisk, is on trial. He says that Stokes's testimony, being more directly self-interested than that of other witnesses, must be treated with greater caution. He reiterates that the killing is not at issue, only the degree of culpability. Stokes can be found guilty of murder in the first degree or manslaughter in the third degree, or the homicide can be judged justifiable. In the strongest language he can muster, Judge Boardman urges the jury to reach a verdict. The question, he says, is a simple one to honest men.

The jury retires at ten past eight in the evening. Few in the audience expect a verdict that night, and most go home. The resolute, however, are rewarded. A little past eleven Judge Boardman returns to the courtroom and takes his place at the bench. The prisoner is brought in. The jury is summoned.

"Gentlemen, have you reached a verdict?" the clerk of the court inquires.

"We have," the foreman answers.

Stokes is ordered to stand. The jury also rises.

"Prisoner, look upon the jury," the clerk directs. "Jury, look upon the prisoner."

The twelve jurors gaze at Stokes. He slowly lifts his eyes toward them.

"Gentlemen of the jury, how say you? Do you find Edward S. Stokes, the prisoner at the bar, guilty or not guilty?"

"Guilty of murder in the first degree."

Stokes shudders. His sister shrieks, but as her voice dies away the room is perfectly still.

After a long frozen moment the jurors sit down. Stokes slumps into his chair. Judge Boardman, appearing relieved and not a little surprised, thanks and discharges the jury.

Stokes's shock gradually turns to anger. He faces the private prosecutor. "Mr. Beach," he says bitterly, "you have done your work well. I hope you have been paid for it."

District Attorney Fellows answers Stokes by declaring that Beach has served reluctantly and without any fee from the family or friends of Jim Fisk.

"Not from Jay Gould?" Stokes demands disbelievingly.

He gets no answer from Beach. Fellows, who thanks his associates for their diligence, says he has had enough of the prosecution business and is retiring. The seamy side of human nature has taken its toll.

Stokes is led toward the door, his anger growing by the second. As he passes Beach, he appears about to fly at his nemesis, and Beach's co-counsel gather around to protect him.

One of the jurors, on exiting, leans over to defense attorney Tremain. "I hope that you do not feel in any way bad against us, as we tried to do our duty," the juror says. "I am sure you did yours, and worked as hard for Stokes as if he was your own son."

"I have nothing to say," Tremain replies. "But how did you stand on the jury?"

"I do not think I have any right to state that, sir," the juror responds.

"Oh, there is no harm," District Attorney Fellows interjects. "Now it is all over you may speak your mind."

"Well, we stood, going out, ten for conviction and two for acquittal."

A junior counsel on Stokes's side blurts out: "Yes, and those two gave in like cravens and cowards."

Tempers flare, and a fistfight seems likely. But Fellows has another purpose. The district attorney approaches Stokes. Tears are seen rolling down the prosecutor's cheeks. He holds out his hand. "Ned, I hope you have no hard feelings against me," he says. "I did only my duty, and did not try to exceed it, as God made me."

Stokes rejects the hand. "I hear all you say, and I suppose you think it's all right," he says. "But a verdict given on perjured testimony is a villainy that no one will countenance—never, never, so long as the world stands."

⟨ 36 ⟩

The news of Stokes's conviction races ahead of him along Centre Street as he is walked back to the Tombs. His fellow prisoners fall silent when he passes their cells. The petty offenders observe him with indifference, but several prisoners held on murder charges appear deeply worried. Conventional wisdom among the malefactors of the city is that a New York jury can never agree on a charge as serious as murder. The counterexample of Stokes gives them sobering pause.

He falls asleep quickly in his private cell and is allowed to slumber the next morning till nine. He washes, eats breakfast, and is readied for the return to the courtroom for sentencing.

The crowds outside the court are larger than ever. They have trampled the wet snow in City Hall Park and made the lawn a morass. They discover that entry into the courtroom is hopeless, as elected and appointed officials of the city and county have claimed all the available seats for themselves and their friends. But hundreds cram into the hallways and vestibules, to be out of the snow and somewhat closer to the events.

Stokes enters at half past ten, better dressed than he has been during the argument phase of the trial. A blue overcoat covers a dark suit; black kid gloves encase his hands. He struggles to hide any emotion; he is steeling himself for the worst.

But his brother, who stands beside him, lacks comparable control. Dressed in black, as if already in mourning, he weeps as if at his brother's funeral. The audience looks on and whispers in amazement.

The entry of Judge Boardman silences the room. The prisoner is asked to stand. "Edward S. Stokes," the clerk inquires, "what have you to say why sentence of death should not be pronounced upon you?"

Stokes answers clearly and deliberately: "I can only say that I am innocent of the crime of which I now stand convicted. I did not intentionally violate any laws of the land." He looks around the court. "I know that all the testimony that was given for the defense was viewed lightly by the jury. I feel convinced of that. I know that public clamor has been aroused against me from the frequent murders in New York City. I know that the evidence of Thomas Hart"—the doorman at the Grand Central Hotel—"upon which I have been convicted, is false from beginning to end. I believe that the prosecution knew it."

He speaks directly to the judge: "That is all I have to say. I hope you will make the sentence as brief as possible."

He turns to sit down, but Tremain touches his elbow to let him know he must continue to stand. Briefly embarrassed, he faces the bench once more.

Judge Boardman looks out on the crowd, the representatives of the people of New York, and then at the prisoner. "You have been defended by the most eminent counsel with extraordinary skill and devotion," the judge says. "You have been supported and sustained by the sympathy of loving relatives and ardent friends. All that wealth, affection, or industry could render has been cheerfully and well done. A jury, carefully selected, of intelligent and upright gentlemen, have listened patiently and kindly to your own account of this most terrible act, as well as to the other evidence that has been put in in your behalf. They have found you guilty of murder in the first degree—the highest crime known in our law—in having caused the death of James Fisk, Jr., one year ago today."

The judge says he concurs in the decision of the jury. He asserts that he has made no errors that he is aware of in determining the admissibility of evidence. He states that he has given the prisoner the benefit of the doubt at every turn of the trial.

One responsibility is left for him to fulfill. "To me remains the painful duty of pronouncing the judgment of the law, not alone as a punishment of your crime, but also that, by your example, others may take warning. I am sad over your unhappy fate—so young, so attractive in person, with so many fountains of joy yet untasted. Still greater is my sorrow to realize the unmerited anguish you have brought upon your family and friends. It is a frightful legacy to leave to a family—a specter that death alone can banish."

The judge speaks very slowly now. "Edward S. Stokes, in obedience to the requirements of the law, this court orders and directs that you be taken hence in the custody of the sheriff of the City and County of New York to the prison from whence you came; that you be there confined in close custody by said sheriff until the 28th day of February, 1873, and that on that day, between the hours of eleven o'clock in the morning and three o'clock in the afternoon, you be hanged by the neck until you are dead. May God have mercy on your soul."

❧ 37 ❧

Stokes is stunned. He is led from the courtroom in a daze and delivered back to the Tombs. The other prisoners avoid him, as though his hopeless condition might be contagious. With the city abuzz at the thought of a hanging, his lawyers' appeals for writs of error meet one rebuff after another. The corridors of his prison grow darker than ever; the specter of the gallows rises before him. Convinced that the forces of Erie and Tammany still determine justice in New York, Ned Stokes surrenders to his fate.

And then, with the hangman almost readying the noose, the New York Supreme Court finds in Stokes's favor. The court rules that the jury in the second trial was incorrectly charged. Judge Boardman failed to make clear that murder, under New York statute, requires an explicit intent to kill. Stokes certainly meant to harm Fisk, but whether he sought to kill him remains unproved, the court says. The conviction is voided; Stokes shall have a third trial.

Stokes's brother carries the glad tidings to the Tombs, wanting to witness and share the emotions of the eleventh-hour rescue. But the jailhouse grapevine relays messages faster than any human courier. A guard tells Stokes he isn't going to hang. Stokes takes a moment to absorb the guard's words and nearly faints as the welcome meaning sinks in. He can't speak, he can't breathe, he can barely hear or see.

Gradually he recomposes himself. By the time his brother arrives, expecting a joyous reaction, Stokes presents the calm, unconcerned persona he has long preferred to show the world.

38

Maybe it is a miracle. Maybe it is justice. Or maybe it is simply coincidence that Stokes's reprieve comes amid the passing of the Erie and Tweed rings.

Fisk's death initially relieved Jay Gould of the liabilities attendant upon Fisk's egregious professional manner and scandalous lifestyle, but it also deprived Gould of his staunchest ally at Erie headquarters. In the year since the murder, several members of the Erie board, in collaboration with dissatisfied shareholders, have mounted a challenge to Gould's reign. They enlist a Civil War general who leads them on a march to the Opera House, where they physically remove Gould from his lavish offices before voting him out of the corporate presidency.

Gould's fall, after Fisk's death, further weakens the third member of their triumvirate, Bill Tweed. Gould furnished the bail that let Tweed sleep at home awaiting his trial on the corruption charges; with Gould's overthrow from Erie, Tweed has to look to his own devices. His lawyers place one hurdle after another in the path of New York justice, but finally Tweed is convicted and sentenced to twelve years in prison.

≋ **39** ≋

The downfall of the Erie and Tweed rings is accompanied by a hurricane in the economy at large. For all the financial shenanigans of Fisk and Gould, the American economy has grown rapidly since the Civil War. But fat years eventually give way to lean, and in the autumn of 1873 the country suffers its first full-blown panic of the industrial era. Jay Cooke—the "good" Jay of Wall Street, renowned and respected for floating the bonds that supported the Union government during the war, in contrast to the bad Jay Gould of the Erie war and the gold conspiracy—finds himself burdened with millions of dollars of Northern Pacific Railroad bonds he can't unload, and when Cooke & Co. closes its doors, the financial markets seize up. The panic spreads to the stock market and then to the economy as a whole. The railroad industry drives over a cliff into massive receivership; factories damp their furnaces and bar their doors; inventories pile up in warehouses; real estate prices collapse; savers lose their nest eggs in bank closures; workers lose their jobs. Panics in preindustrial America were sometimes sharp but never long or especially wide. When the nation's economy rested on agriculture, people could always eat from their own gardens even if they couldn't buy from their neighbors, and they could live in their own houses even if they couldn't afford to paint or repair them. Now that the economy depends on industry, downturns are far more devastating. Laid-off workers lack money for food and rent; they and their families soon find themselves hungry and homeless. And the growing interconnectedness of the economy causes panics to ramify far from their origins. No one knows it in 1873, but the panic of this year will produce a nationwide depression lasting the rest of the decade, with bloody strife setting labor against management and political divisions pitting one half of the country against the other half.

∾ **40** ∾

Stokes's third trial commences a month into the panic, and with the papers filled with dreadful economic news, it draws far less attention than the first and second trials. The primary novel evidence is a statement by a witness the defense has found who says he saw a pistol in Fisk's hand at the time of the shooting. The prosecution challenges the statement—Why has the witness surfaced only now? Why can't he remember more details of the event?—but in other respects the trial tracks the two previous ones.

The jury this time, more carefully charged than the last, yields a verdict finally favorable, in a comparative sense, to Stokes. He is convicted of manslaughter in the third degree rather than murder in the first. The sentence is four years in prison rather than death.

41

"In the list of murders which have disgraced the annals of this City for a score of years," a graybeard of the fourth estate reflects in sending Stokes off to Sing Sing, "none created a greater excitement than the shooting of James Fisk, Jr., by Edward S. Stokes. Both men had their warm partisans and enemies, and both enjoyed a national celebrity—a celebrity of a character not worthy of emulation. On the one side James Fisk, brilliant, unscrupulous, immoral, and debonair, the beau ideal of the fast, shrewd, go-ahead speculator; on the other hand, Edward S. Stokes, reared in affluence, accustomed to have every impulse and wish gratified, every object obtained. Between them Helen Josephine Mansfield Lawlor, the Aspasia who, by the bending of her thumb, like Nero's wife, Agrippina, brought the conflict of the arena to a fatal conclusion."

Fisk is gone forever, Stokes for the term of his sentence, and Josie . . . ?

Josie has vanished. Amid the legal wrangling over Stokes's fate she slipped out of her house on Twenty-third Street and out of the city she turned upside down. Competing rumors put her in contradictory places, but the most plausible indicate an extended European tour. English and some French papers have followed the Fisk murder and the Stokes trials, but Josie's profile is far lower overseas than in America, and she can hope to disappear among the many other travelers who, in the age of steamships and railroads, are helping launch the modern tourist industry.

42

Stokes isn't constituted for prison life. Sing Sing makes the Tombs look like a health spa, and within months he suffers respiratory ailments that cause the authorities to fear for his survival. They move him to a medical facility at Auburn, where he revives sufficiently to boast to visitors that he is speculating in stocks. He claims to have cleared thirty thousand dollars in recent transactions. He applies for a pardon to Governor Tilden, hoping the anti-Tammany chief executive will look mercifully on his case. But Tilden, whose ambitions have moved beyond breaking Bill Tweed and the Tammany ring to running for president, has no desire to dredge up old scandals. Yet Stokes still manages to exit prison early. His physical condition declines again, and in October 1876, three years into his four-year sentence, he is granted a medical discharge.

Bill Tweed has no such luck. The Tammany boss manages to get his twelve-year criminal sentence reduced to one year, but he is quickly brought up on a civil suit and reconfined, for debt. He posts bail and then jumps it, fleeing the country to Cuba. By the time he is traced there, he has shipped out for Spain. Spanish authorities discover and arrest him—using, reportedly, a Thomas Nast cartoon for identification—and extradite him back to America. Returned to the Ludlow Street jail, in the heart of the city he once ruled, mere blocks from the court-house that remains his monument to corruption, forgotten by Tammany Hall, which has moved on without him, Bill Tweed contracts pneumonia and in 1878 breathes his last.

Jay Gould exhibits greater staying power. After the death of Fisk and the fall of Tweed, Gould gradually regains his financial touch, building a railroad empire in the West and adjoining it to the Western Union telegraph network. His accomplishments win him applause from many of those his enterprises employ, but the old enmities die hard, and his 1892 passing inspires reflection on his days at Erie. "The example he set is a dangerous one to follow," the *New York Herald* warns. The *World* calls Gould "one of the most sinister figures that ever flitted bat-like across the vision of the American people."

Stokes reaches the new century but is largely forgotten. He never recaptures the insouciance of his youth, and even the affected nonchalance of certain moments of his post-Fisk phase is more than he can sustain. Friends find him fearful, often paranoid; he seems to think the ghost of Fisk is on his trail. He tries his hand at the hotel trade, purchasing the Hoffman House, his residence at the time of the shooting, but he has to sell it a few years later. He develops kidney disease and dies in November 1901, while America is reeling from another shocking murder, of President William McKinley at Buffalo, which brings the Gilded Age to a belated but resounding close.

43

Josie outlasts them all. She remains in Europe for several years, marrying an American lawyer in London in 1891. He seems to love her, not least because, as he tells a visitor, she is the only woman who can save him from drinking himself to death. But she can't save him from drinking himself insane, and she divorces him for mental incapacity. She returns to Boston, and then Philadelphia. At least one news story puts her in South Dakota. She is said to be an invalid, or in a convent. Several papers report her death.

Yet she carries on. She crosses the ocean again to Europe, eventually settling in Paris. How she supports herself none can say; her charms are less obvious than they were when she drove Jim Fisk to distraction and Ned Stokes to murder. But something persists, and when her end finally comes, almost sixty years after that fatal meeting on the staircase of the Grand Central Hotel, one devoted acquaintance—the heir to Fisk, or is it to Stokes?—follows her casket to the burial site on Montparnasse and bids Josie Mansfield earthly farewell.

❦ Sources ❦

The story just rendered is true. The characters and events were real; the words attributed to them were their own. Their actions and statements were recorded contemporaneously by journalists and other observers and related at length. New York's many newspapers, including such major papers as the *Herald,* the *Tribune,* the *Times,* and the *World,* and smaller papers like the *Irish World,* provided blow-by-blow and word-by-word coverage of Jim Fisk, Josie Mansfield, Ned Stokes, Jay Gould, Daniel Drew, Cornelius Vanderbilt, and William Tweed. Legal depositions, trial transcripts, and summaries of court proceedings were published in various editions at the time and later. The Erie war and Black Friday triggered probes that culminated in published exposés, most notably *Chapters of Erie,* by Henry Adams and Charles Francis Adams, Jr., and *Investigation into the Causes of the Gold Panic,* by the Banking and Currency Committee of the House of Representatives. Context on the speculations and peculations of Fisk, Gould, Tweed, and their ilk comes from the large historical literature on the Gilded Age, to which the present author's *American Colossus: The Triumph of Capitalism, 1865–1900,* affords an up-to-date entrée.